Charlotte's Table

Charlotte's Table

Down Home Cooking from an Uptown Girl

CHARLOTTE ARMSTRONG

THE ECCO PRESS

THE ECCO PRESS
100 West Broad Street
Hopewell, New Jersey 08525

Published simultaneously in Canada by
Penguin Books Canada Ltd., Ontario
Printed in the United States of America

LIBRARY OF CONGRESS CATALOGING-IN-PUBLICATION DATA
    Armstrong, Charlotte, 1963–
    Charlotte's table: down home cooking from an uptown girl /
Charlotte Armstrong. — 1st ed.
        p.   cm.
    Includes index.
    ISBN 0-88001-545-4
    1. Cookery, American—Louisiana style. 2. Cookery—
Louisiana—New Orleans.   1. Title.
TX715.2.L68A76   1998
641.59763—dc21   97-22335

Designed by Susanna Gilbert, The Typeworks
The text of this book is set in Janson Text

9 8 7 6 5 4 3 2 1

FIRST EDITION 1998

To Melda LaChute &
Etta Mae Armstrong,
with love.

Acknowledgments

Writing this book has been my most challenging and rewarding labor of love to date, and I am indebted to each of you who have helped me along the way these past two years. I am particularly grateful to those who so generously shared recipes and culinary secrets, for much of this book relies on collective wisdom and knowledge. My special thanks goes to those listed below, all of whom have played major parts in the realization of this book:

MaMa Armstrong and MaMa LaChute, for nourishing me with your love of cooking.

Stephen and Cathy, for your consistent enthusiasm for the work I've done in your kitchen and for your blessing on this project.

Daniel Halpern, for loving my food so much that you were able to see a book in me.

Vera, Chip, Johanna, Bruno, Max, and Sara, for being undying sources of support and love each in your own way.

Mom, for always telling me I could do anything I put my mind to.

Daddy, for showing me how important it is to do something you love.

Crista, for being the best sister-friend-critic anyone could ever want.

Judy Capodanno, for gently steering me and my words in the right direction.

It goes without saying that without my family heritage this book would not be. My greatest joy in writing this book was the realization of the rich legacy I inherited.

Thank you.

Contents

Introduction

As a food professional, I guess it's not surprising that when I review my life to date, it flashes back to me as a series of memorable moments inextricably bound by food. There are many important events in my life that I cannot recall. However, ask me about my first oyster, the Mile High Pie Mom used to take us for at the Pontchartrain Hotel, or my first experience with foie gras (my date thought I was having an out of body experience), and I can expound at length and in great, animated detail. The same is true of places I've visited. I can tap into moments centered around food with ease and intensity: my introduction to Stilton cheese in London (by far the best thing that happened to me there), eating koshary on the streets of Cairo with my sister, the incomparable sweetness of lobster speared off the coast of Belize and grilled right there on the beach. I certainly have other significant memories of the places I've been, but food is often the vehicle that touches something very central to who I am. When food is involved, the experience always makes a strong imprint on me.

Food is powerful. It nurtures, sustains, and comforts us in ways nothing else does. It tells us stories about where it comes from and, sometimes, where *we* come from. It crosses boundaries of language and culture. It communicates for us when sometimes we can't. It takes us places we've never been and brings us back to places we'd like to be again. Food speaks.

I realize that not everyone feels this way about food. I have been told there are those among us who just eat to live. A difficult concept for me to digest, indeed. I consider myself quite fortunate to have such an integral connection to one of life's simple pleasures, as well as to have this passion be my profession.

Having grown up in New Orleans, a city where the culinary

climate is as intense as the geographical one, certainly predisposed me to feeling this way about food and provided me with a wealth of incredible food experiences. New Orleanians consider it a sin to eat bad food—a philosophy I subscribe to heartily. The unique combination of cultures that flavor New Orleans and her food serve as a backdrop for my palate—a canvas from which to work. From the French we inherited rich sauces, impeccable technique, and a learned reverence for food. The Spanish combined their contribution with the Creole Island influences to give us spice and heat, and from our African forefathers we were brought things like okra and the word "gumbo," which has taken on a life all its own. Later, Cajun, Italian, German, and Irish immigrants brought their own particular tastes to the city's already fecund food scene. Together with the tropical climate, perfect for growing integral vegetables and seasonings, and her location right on the banks of the Mississippi, just a few miles upstream from the incredibly fertile river delta, New Orleans has clearly had a tremendous culinary advantage. Louisiana's transplanted peoples all seemed to find refuge in her bayous and backwoods, and the Cajun and Italian communities particularly thrived, finding it easy to cultivate and obtain the food products essential to their particular cuisines. Boundaries between communities became less and less clear, and the rich New Orleans culinary legacy grew into its own. It is easy to see all of these influences in the food of New Orleans today—and equally difficult to categorize a particular dish, taste, or flavor as being representative of only one of these contributors. New Orleans food, like her character, is the result of this myriad of influences that have converged upon her over the years. Complex yet simple, spicy yet not always, provincial and refined at the same time.

The two gems in my culinary upbringing are my grandmothers, Melda LaChute and Etta Mae Armstrong, whom I refer to as MaMa LaChute and MaMa Armstrong. Though they are of very different worlds, they are both exceptional cooks and have passed down to me their love of food and feeding others.

MaMa LaChute was raised south of New Orleans on a bayou

so small it has no name, in Point-a-la-Hache, Louisiana. Her family was a mixture of Cajun and Italian, like most folks down there, and her food is reflective of that heritage. As many in the family have made their living off the land, mostly fishing, shrimping, or trawling, seafood figures predominantly in her repertoire. She has an innate ability to season to perfection. The backbone of her cooking philosophy is simple: Don't hold back. To witness the amount of onion, garlic, and hot pepper she cooks with can be startling for someone not yet initiated, but her food is never heavy-handed, her seasoning is always just enough to complement, not disguise, the basic flavors of the dish. Her combination of seasonings is simple and traditional, and yet she just has the touch. She recently remarked to me how someone in the family wanted to know why their sauce never tasted like hers, and she laughed, telling me, "Well, what do they expect when they start with only half an onion and no garlic?"

MaMa Armstrong comes from a tiny little town in Louisiana called Melville. This is not far from Opelousas, a town considered by some to be the heart of Cajun country. She is not Cajun, however. Her family is of English and Irish descent, and from what I know (and can tell by their accents), they've been in the South for quite some time. She is what I would call "southern" southern—and does things the "southern" way—vegetables cooked beyond recognition (but oh, so good), most things "smothered," and lots of bacon drippings involved in all. Lots of pork any way you can imagine it, and many things fried. Southern food is simple food, usually cooked a long time and almost always flavored by pork in any of its guises, whether it is smoked, salt cured, or pickled. At MaMa's table, almost every meal is accompanied by hot cornbread or cornsticks to dip into the cooking juices left on your plate. That, and lots of rice and gravy.

From watching both MaMas I learned the basics: how to make a roux, how to not be shy about seasonings, how enjoyable it can be to stand over a pot of simmering something, communing with it until it has become what you've envisioned. The best thing I learned, however, was how rewarding it can be to put something on the table in front of someone and help them on to one of their own food moments. This is what I want to share with you.

The recipes I've chosen to include are an eclectic bunch: both familiar and cosmopolitan, elementary as well as a bit more advanced, mild and spicy, rich and lean. In a way, they are my history: representatives of where I come from, where I've been, where I long to go, where I've worked, and whose homes I've eaten in along the way. I hope they strike some chords in you.

Some Things to Consider

To help you successfully create a food moment of your own, there are a few things I'd like to say about some basic yet important concepts:

The Perfect Roux

First and foremost, there is roux and then there is roux. A roux is a mixture of some sort of fat with flour, which when cooked and added to a liquid will perform as a thickening agent. Rouxs are especially important in Creole, Cajun, and southern cooking, where they are used frequently and serve as the backbone of any number of dishes, such as bisques, étouffées, and gumbos. They contribute a rich, earthy flavor and give substance and texture to an otherwise thin stock, soup, or gravy. What many people do not realize is how careful one must be when cooking a roux, and, sometimes, how long it can take. The length of time necessary will depend on the amount of roux you are preparing, as well as on the specific color roux you have in mind. Cajun folks sometimes cook their roux so dark that anyone else would think it was beyond hope. My chef instructor in cooking school showed me what he called a "dark" roux, and added that anything darker would render the food completely indigestible. Well, folks, let me tell you that many in the Cajun community are enjoying these so-called "indigestible" rouxs at this moment, have been for years, and will continue to for a long time to come.

Cooking a roux is not difficult, but it does require time and your complete attention. The first thing to realize when you plan to make a roux is that you should have nothing else to do for the duration of the process. And by this I mean exactly what I say: nothing else whatsoever. If the phone rings, let it ring. If you have a child, he or she should be sleeping soundly. For, if for one moment you decide to discontinue the constant stirring that is necessary for a successful roux, odds are your roux will suffer for it. Once it is even a tiny bit burned, a roux will taste burned through and through. Constant stirring in a heavy pot, such as a cast-iron skillet, over medium-high heat should lead you to a successful roux. Second, don't be afraid to cook a roux long enough. If a recipe calls for a dark roux, in my book that means milk chocolate brown. Medium is close to a caramel color. Light would be a blond color. The longer a roux is cooked and the darker it becomes, the earthier, more complex a flavor it will impart to a dish. The choice of fat you use will also have an effect on the flavor. (I always use butter, because I think it provides such a nice, nutty flavor. Those with heart concerns can easily substitute canola oil for the butter, if desired.) You will see that the roux goes through many different stages as it cooks, at times appearing very smooth and at times rather clotted. This is normal. The smell can guide you, too. You will learn to recognize the point at which the pleasant popcorn smell just starts to turn to a burned smell when the cooking of a dark roux nears its end.

Also, note that many of the recipes that follow call for you to add chopped seasoning vegetables to the roux when it has reached the appropriate stage—this is a perfect way to cool off your roux so that it will not continue to color. It also almost instantly sautés your seasoning vegetables. And finally, remember that next to a sugar burn, a hot oil burn is the most dangerous burn you can get in the kitchen. Be very careful when stirring a roux. I have learned that it is better to be warm and have as much flesh as possible covered when stirring a roux than to be cool and exposed. The hot grease goes through many stages as it cooks, and at some moments it is very liquid and easily splattered. Do take care. With all that said—rouxs don't need to be feared.

Soulful Seasoning

One thing I have taken with me from my formative years in New Orleans is an intimate relationship with what New Orleanians refer to as "the trinity." The only religious significance here is the belief in starting almost every dish with three specific ingredients: onion, celery, and bell pepper. I have taken it a step further, and have a personal belief in the trinity plus one—beloved garlic. You will see that many of my recipes begin with sautéing these three or four ingredients. (I am less enamored with bell pepper than some New Orleanian cooks, for I feel it can sometimes dominate the flavor of a dish if it is used too freely. A little goes a long way, unless you're preparing something like Shrimp Creole, in which the pepper flavor should be a significant one.) Generally speaking, however, these four ingredients, used in appropriate ratios (you will see that this becomes a personal judgment) provide you with an excellent base of seasoning in almost everything you cook. I suggest you get on good terms with the trinity plus one.

Herbs and spices are also important, as they are what sometimes bring all the different elements of a dish together. With experience comes the knowledge of which spices or herbs complement particular foods, as well as which spices find a happy home on your palate. I have a well-developed fondness for basil, thyme, bay laurel, rosemary, parsley, red pepper, and cayenne—these are all used regularly in New Orleans cooking. There are other herbs and spices that have piqued my interest since leaving home and are now indispensable to me: cilantro, ginger, sage, sesame, cumin, chili powder, turmeric, allspice, cloves, and cinnamon. These all have special places in my cooking, and I rely on them all to strut their stuff in my food.

One of Louisiana's seasoning secrets is Tony Chachere's Creole Seasoning. Though I generally do not like spice blends or seasoned salts, I would be lost without "Tony's," as I and many other New Orleanians refer to it. It is a blend of salt, cayenne pepper, and other spices, which Tony's has combined in the most perfect proportions, with no MSG. It claims to be "Great On

Everything" and it truly is. I know many who use it as they would table salt. I find that it makes almost anything taste better, and if a dish seems to be missing something and I can't quite put my finger on what that something is, often just a dash of Tony's will make all the difference. One thing to note is that it does contain salt, so if you opt to use it freely, do adjust the inclusion of salt to make up for this. If you live in the South, odds are you already know Tony's. If not, and you have trouble finding it, call their hotline number at 1-800-551-9066.

The Magic of Bacon

Let's talk about bacon. Relax. I know that in this modern world of health concerns and information on nutrition, the thought of having bacon in any way, shape, or form is clearly forbidden. Well, I'm here to tell you to just go for it. Every now and then, that is. I am a firm believer in moderation, not to mention the law of supply and demand. According to what I've seen of human nature, if our body is craving something one day and it is not allowed to have it, then, more times than not, we overload the following day. A yen for smothered green beans, flavored with that indescribable bacon smokiness one day, gone unanswered, might mean an unplanned binge on a hot fudge sundae the next. So listen to your body and—occasionally—treat yourself.

In the South, it is a custom to keep a jar or can on or near the stove with the sole function of collecting unused bacon grease. Whenever bacon is cooked, the grease is just emptied into the container. Then you don't have to fry bacon when all you really need is a little grease for flavor. If you plan to use the reserved bacon grease with any sort of regularity, it can simply be stored, covered, at room temperature. If you are less likely to use it in a timely manner, simply store it, covered, in the refrigerator, where it can be kept almost indefinitely. In the following recipes you can substitute a tablespoon or two of bacon grease, or even less if you're really trying to be good, for the actual bacon. A little bacon is better than none at all, as the flavor is, indisputably, unrivaled.

Stocks

As most serious cooks know, a well-tended, homemade stock is always superior to storebought bouillon cubes or canned stock. You will then, perhaps, wonder why many of my recipes call for bouillon cubes. The simple answer is time. In the work I do there are simply not enough hours in the day for me to make my own stocks as well as prepare all the meals. My guess is that many of you will be under the same duress. In certain dishes, the addition of one or two bouillon cubes will provide just the right amount of flavor without compromising the taste or quality of the end result. In other recipes flavors can be subtle, and in these cases I feel a homemade stock is necessary to the integrity of the dish. By all means, if you do have the time, make your own stocks and simply substitute them for the bouillon cubes and some of the liquid called for in the recipe.

All that is necessary for successful homemade stocks is a little forethought and the time necessary for gentle simmering. If you have the space in your freezer, I suggest making an effort to prepare your own stocks and store them there, in small portions. They can then be pulled out and used as necessary.

To make homemade stocks, take advantage of the remainders of roast meats and chickens. All one needs to do is throw these leftovers into a large pot with a carrot or two, a couple stalks of celery, an onion, several cloves of garlic, some stray parsley stems, and a bit of black or red pepper. The vegetables don't even need to be peeled. Bring all of this to a boil in a large pot with plenty of fresh cold water to cover the ingredients, skim away any scum that rises to the surface, reduce the heat to a simmer and let the rest happen by itself. A chicken stock only needs to simmer about 2 hours. For beef, veal, or lamb, 4 or 5 hours should be sufficient to extract flavor from the bones. Stocks should be strained through a fine sieve and allowed to cool completely before refrigerating or freezing.

You can play around with stocks, too. If you want a richer stock, try browning the bones and vegetables in the oven before simmering. Also, note that sometimes a fresh tomato can add an interesting note to beef or lamb stocks. If you opt to get serious about stocks, consult your butcher, and he or she will no doubt steer you in the right direction as to which cuts of meat and which bones particularly make the best stocks. Fortunately, it is the least expensive cuts of meat and sometimes the leftover parts that are traditionally used for stocks, so the cost involved is minimal.

If you opt to use bouillon cubes, try different brands. The tastes vary greatly, and once you have determined your favorite, you can be sure of a consistent flavor. There is a wonderful family-owned and -operated spice mail-order company, The Spice House, that offers several different excellent soup bases. If you are sensitive to MSG, which is often found in store-bought bouillon cubes, The Spice House has delicious soup bases that are MSG free. If you are on a sodium-restricted diet, they also have salt-free bases available, as well as high-quality herbs and spices, all at reasonable prices. They can be reached by phone at (414) 272-0977, or by mail at 1031 N. Old World Third Street, Milwaukee, Wisconsin 53203.

A Note to My Vegetarian Friends

To those of you who choose this way of life, I respect your choice and ask that you not feel there is little here for you. Though many of the recipes do contain meat, many may also be altered for a vegetarian palate—especially those recipes in which meat is used to flavor vegetables, in which case the meat may simply be omitted. If you are not used to eating meat, the flavor will not be missed. Many of the soups can easily be altered as well, simply by substituting vegetable stock or bouillon cubes for the chicken or beef stock specified in the recipe. Real bacon may be replaced by turkey bacon for some of you, and there are several soy- and tofu-based products available in the supermarkets these days for those of you who eat no meat at all. The flavor is not exactly the same, but is nevertheless an excellent substitute for the richness that meatless food sometimes lacks.

❊ ❊ ❊

Now that you're armed with the basics, remember that the most authentic southern thing you can do is enjoy the recipes. Change them if you are so inclined. Experiment! Remember to relax and appreciate the process of cooking. It can be such a rewarding labor of love, as I have learned, and is transferred to those lucky enough to sit at your table with you. Hospitality needn't be practiced—it is always felt when you open your door to others to share the simple ritual of a home-cooked meal. Remember—the kitchen can be your place of creative liberation: Don't hold back!

Charlotte's Table

Bold Beginnings
& Simmering Soups

It seems that bold is the way to begin, as, in much of life, first impressions seem to carry the most weight. The first course sets the tone of a meal and also leaves its mark on the diner's memory simply because it is the first taste to assuage the hungry palate. It is with this in mind that I have chosen this selection of recipes to begin a meal. I've also included an entourage of soups that can be used to start a meal, or as meals unto themselves.

Soups are my very favorite things to cook. I think it might go back to my childhood . . . I have such pleasant memories of looking up to my grandmothers as they stood and stirred and leaned their heads over simmering pots of assorted ingredients. It could also have something to do with my frugal side, as soups are one of the best ways to clean out the refrigerator. It is a great sense of accomplishment to make something wonderful out of bits and pieces of this and that—leftovers, abandoned bones, or assorted vegetables. I feel most creatively challenged when I cook this way, and some of my most applauded creations hail from kitchen cleanup times. If you find you are missing a soup ingredient, don't worry. Look to your pantry, open your refrigerator. Odds are you have something you can substitute. Soups are forgiving this way, unlike pastry recipes, which are far more precise.

The recipe yields in this section are for first courses or appetizers, although many of the recipes are substantial enough to serve as light entrées. If you choose to serve one of these recipes as a main course, simply divide the yield in half for an approximate number of main-course servings.

Bold Beginnings

Chicken Liver Ravioli with Brown Butter and Fresh Sage
Crista's Hummus
Oyster Pan Roast
Pan-Seared Portobello Mushrooms
with Garlic-Infused Olive Oil
Potato Pancakes with Smoked Salmon and Scallion Cream
MaMa LaChute's Shrimp Patties
Craig's Truffle Risotto
Grilled Vegetable Napoleons with Basil Vinaigrette

Chicken Liver Ravioli with Brown Butter and Fresh Sage

If you love ravioli the way I do and also happen to be a liver lover, throw caution to the winds with this one: The chicken liver filling is quickly sautéed and flavored with Cognac, fresh herbs, and Parmesan cheese. Thin gyoza skins make great ravioli cases, and with nutty brown butter perfumed by fresh sage leaves, topped with more Parmesan and some crispy apple cubes, this is definitely a sensual experience—the closest you can get to foie gras without the real thing.

The gyoza skins are what Asian restaurants use for spring rolls or dumplings, and they happen to make a very good, light ravioli shell. The great thing about the gyoza skins is that they are of uniform thickness, are precut, and cook very quickly. You can find them in most Asian grocery stores, but if you cannot get hold of any, egg roll wrappers or wonton skins work well, as do fresh pasta sheets, which you can often buy at Italian specialty stores or in the freezer section of some supermarkets.

Although I've suggested this as a first course (perfect before roast chicken or duck), it also makes a wonderful entrée.

Filling

3 slices bacon
3 shallots, finely chopped
2 tablespoons butter
2 cloves garlic, pressed or minced
1 pound chicken livers, rinsed and patted dry
1 teaspoon finely chopped fresh thyme or ½ teaspoon dried, crumbled
1 teaspoon chopped fresh sage or ½ teaspoon dried, crumbled
2 tablespoons Cognac or brandy
2 tablespoons heavy cream
⅔ cup finely grated Parmigiano-Reggiano cheese
½ teaspoon salt, or to taste
Freshly ground black pepper, to taste

1 10-ounce package gyoza skins (about 50 skins)
1 large egg white

Garnish

8 tablespoons salted butter
12 to 15 fresh sage leaves
½ cup freshly grated Parmigiano-Reggiano cheese
2 teaspoons fresh thyme leaves
1 Golden Delicious apple, peeled, cored, and cut
   into ¼-inch cubes

In a large skillet, cook the bacon over medium heat until almost crisp and most of its fat has been rendered. Remove the bacon and discard or save for another purpose. Add the shallots, butter, garlic, chicken livers, thyme, and sage to the skillet and sauté, stirring occasionally, until the shallots are tender and the chicken livers are lightly browned on all sides but still pink in the center, about 5 minutes. Add the Cognac and continue to cook until most of the liquid has evaporated.

In a food processor, purée the cooked chicken livers with the heavy cream. Pour into another bowl and stir in the grated cheese. Season with salt and pepper. (Slight overseasoning is in order, to compensate for the pasta that will surround the filling.) Refrigerate until cool, 45 minutes to 1 hour.

When the filling has cooled completely, remove 24 gyoza skins from their packaging. Lay them out on a clean, dry surface. Place a heaping tablespoon of liver mixture in the center of each gyoza skin. Using your fingers, wet the edges of the gyoza skins with egg white. Using the remaining gyoza skins from the package, place a gyoza skin directly on top of each filled skin, and carefully press the edges together, easing the edges to accommodate the filling. Try to seal with as little air inside the ravioli as possible. Set the ravioli aside, covered and refrigerated, until ready to serve.

Fill a large saucepan or kettle three-fourths full of salted water and bring to a boil.

While waiting for the water to boil, heat a large skillet over medium-high heat. When the skillet is very hot, add the salted butter and let it melt in one spot. (Do not move the pan.) When the butter has begun to brown around the edges, pick up the skillet and swirl the contents to keep the melted butter from burning and to melt the remaining butter. Add the sage leaves and reduce the heat to medium. Let cook until the leaves are crispy, 1 to 2 minutes. Remove from the heat and set aside while you cook the ravioli.

Gently add the ravioli to the boiling water and simmer gently until they are floating on the surface, 3 to 4 minutes. Check one to make sure the pasta is cooked all the way through. Serve immediately, garnished with the sage, brown butter, grated cheese, fresh thyme leaves, and cubed apple.

MAKES APPROXIMATELY 24 RAVIOLI, SERVING 6 TO 8 AS AN APPETIZER OR 4 AS A MAIN COURSE

Crista's Hummus

My sister Crista lived in Egypt for two years, and while she was there she learned to cook many Middle Eastern vegetarian dishes. Hummus is just one of them, but one I believe she makes exceptionally well. It is a great dish for a party, as it can be made up to two days in advance and the flavor actually improves overnight. If you do opt to make it in advance, it may need to be seasoned with a bit more salt, and will usually need to be thinned with a tablespoon or two of water before serving. Though I suggest serving it with pita chips, it is also excellent with fresh pitas and vegetable crudités.

2 cans (15½ ounces each) chickpeas, drained
½ cup extra-virgin olive oil
Juice of 1½ lemons
1½ teaspoons ground cumin
1 small onion, chopped
2 cloves garlic, pressed or minced
½ cup water
½ cup tahini
1½ teaspoons salt
¼ teaspoon crushed red pepper
Tony Chachere's Creole Seasoning, to taste
1 tablespoon red wine vinegar
½ red onion, thinly sliced lengthwise, for garnish
Pita chips, for serving

Combine half of the chickpeas with ¼ cup of the oil, the juice of 1 lemon, and the remaining ingredients except the red onion and the pita chips, and process in a food processor until smooth. Add the remaining chickpeas and process briefly, leaving bits of chickpeas visible. Taste and adjust the seasoning, if necessary.

Serve in a shallow bowl or dish, topped with the red onion slivers and drizzled with the remaining ¼ cup oil and the juice of half a lemon. Serve with the pita chips.

SERVES 4 TO 6

Oyster Pan Roast

You can find Oyster Pan Roast on the menus of many New Orleans eating establishments, but this version is inspired by a dish I had at Mosca's, located about fifteen miles outside of New Orleans on Highway 90, when I was a child. It really is too bad that it was so long ago, because I have no idea how they made it or what exactly went into it—I remember richness, garlic, and just-cooked oysters in lots of butter. The recipe below matches my memory.

Though I have suggested this as an appetizer, it also works well as an entrée, served with cooked white rice or pasta and a loaf of hot, crusty French bread.

8 tablespoons (1 stick) butter
¼ cup olive oil
2 bunches scallions, chopped
1 medium rib celery, finely chopped
6 cloves garlic, pressed or minced
2 bay leaves
½ teaspoon dried thyme, crumbled
½ teaspoon dried oregano, crumbled
½ teaspoon dried rosemary, crumbled
4 dozen oysters, shucked and well drained
¼ cup heavy cream
½ cup chopped fresh parsley
Salt (this will depend on the saltiness of the oysters) and
    freshly ground black pepper, to taste
Tony Chachere's Creole Seasoning, to taste
½ cup unseasoned fine dry bread crumbs

Preheat the broiler.

In a large skillet or low-sided saucepan, melt the butter with the olive oil over low heat. Add the scallions, celery, garlic, bay leaves, thyme, oregano, and rosemary. Continue to cook over low heat until the vegetables are tender, about 5 minutes.

Add the drained oysters and stir well to combine with the vegetables. When the oysters just begin to firm up (about 3 to 4 minutes), stir in the heavy cream and parsley and remove from the heat. Taste and season with salt, pepper, and creole seasoning. Place the contents of the skillet in a shallow baking dish (individual ramekins may be used for a more formal presentation). Sprinkle a thin layer of bread crumbs over all and broil 6 inches from the heat source, until the oysters are cooked through and bread crumbs are lightly browned (about 4 to 6 minutes).

SERVES 8 AS AN APPETIZER

Pan-Seared Portobello Mushrooms with Garlic-Infused Olive Oil

> Portobello mushrooms are in a class all their own. With single portobellos sometimes weighing in at over 1 pound each, their size alone tells you they are special. Their hearty flavor and firm texture lend them well to many different recipes, but I think that they are best highlighted in the simple preparation below, which allows the mushroom to be the center of attention.

½ cup extra-virgin olive oil
3 cloves garlic, pressed or minced
4 portobello mushrooms (10 to 12 ounces each), stem ends
  trimmed
Tony Chachere's Creole Seasoning, to taste
Freshly ground black pepper, to taste
½ cup canola or light olive oil
2 tablespoons balsamic vinegar
2 tablespoons chopped fresh herbs of choice, such as basil,
  thyme, summer savory, or rosemary (optional)

Combine the extra-virgin olive oil and garlic in a small bowl and stir well to mix. Let stand at room temperature at least 1 hour and up to 1 day before using.

Slice the mushrooms lengthwise into ⅜-inch slices.

Heat a large skillet over medium-high heat and add 3 tablespoons of oil. When oil is hot but not smoking, add as many mushroom slices as will fit in the skillet in one layer. Sprinkle lightly with the creole seasoning and sauté 2 to 3 minutes, until mushrooms have begun to soften and are seared golden brown on the bottom edges. Turn the mushrooms and drizzle with 2 or 3 tablespoons additional oil. Sauté 2 to 3 minutes, until tender and golden-brown around edges. Remove the mushrooms from the skillet and set aside, lightly covered with foil, while you repeat the cooking process with remaining mushroom slices.

Arrange the mushrooms on a large platter or on individual plates and drizzle with the reserved garlic oil. Drizzle lightly with balsamic vinegar and season with freshly ground black pepper, if desired. Garnish with chopped fresh herbs if available and serve immediately.

SERVES 4 TO 6

Potato Pancakes with Smoked Salmon and Scallion Cream

I daresay most of us have had the pleasure of a crispy potato pancake lathered with sour cream, but try taking it two steps further by adding a slice of smoked salmon and enriching the sour cream with cream cheese, scallions, and lemon zest for a truly memorable taste sensation.

Pancakes

5 Idaho potatoes (about 2 pounds), peeled and coarsely grated
1 teaspoon salt
1 medium onion, grated
2 large eggs
3 tablespoons all-purpose flour
Salt and freshly ground black pepper, to taste
1 to 1½ cups canola oil

Scallion Cream

4 ounces cream cheese, at room temperature
½ cup sour cream, at room temperature
2 scallions, finely chopped
Zest from half a lemon (about ½ teaspoon)
Freshly ground black pepper, to taste
¼ teaspoon salt

8 ounces sliced smoked salmon (about 12 thin slices)
Fresh dill sprigs or snipped fresh chives, for garnish
Lemon wedges, for garnish

Place the grated potatoes in a large colander and sprinkle with salt. Toss briefly to mix, then let the potatoes stand for 15 minutes. Quickly rinse the potatoes under cold water to rinse away any discoloration, then squeeze the potatoes with your hands to remove as much liquid as possible. Combine in a medium bowl with all the remaining pancake ingredients except the oil and set aside.

Preheat the oven to 225°F.

Combine all the ingredients for the scallion cream and whisk vigorously to blend until smooth. Set aside.

In a large skillet, heat ½ cup of the oil until hot but not smoking. Using a ¼-cup measure, scoop ¼-cupfuls of the potato mixture into the skillet and press quickly with a spoon or fork to spread it out to an even ½-inch thickness. Repeat until the skillet is filled, but make sure to leave space between the pancakes so they do not stick together. Cook until golden brown and crispy on both sides, about 2 to 3 minutes per side. Remove with a slotted spoon or spatula to paper towels to drain briefly. Transfer to a baking sheet and keep warm in oven while cooking remaining pancakes, adding more oil as necessary.

Serve each pancake topped with a dollop of scallion cream, with a slice of smoked salmon decoratively arranged on top. Garnish with sprigs of fresh dill or snipped chives and a lemon wedge.

MAKES 12 TO 15 PANCAKES, SERVING 6

MaMa LaChute's Shrimp Patties

This is one of MaMa LaChute's specialties. Though I am told no one can make them quite like she does, I think these get pretty close. Shrimp patties can be served as the beginning to a meal, as below, as a main course with cooked white rice, or as hors d'oeuvres (simply form smaller patties). The batter can be made in advance and even frozen, then fried just before serving. As with almost anything that is fried, these are best when served immediately.

1½ pounds medium shrimp, peeled, deveined, and finely chopped

2 large eggs

1 medium onion, minced

6 cloves garlic, pressed or minced

3 tablespoons chopped fresh parsley

¾ cup unseasoned dry bread crumbs

1 jalapeño or serrano pepper, seeded and finely chopped (wear gloves please!)

½ teaspoon salt, or to taste

1½ cups vegetable or canola oil

Combine all the ingredients except the oil in a large bowl and mix thoroughly. Refrigerate until ready to fry.

In a large skillet, heat the oil over medium-high heat until very hot but not smoking. Drop the batter by heaping tablespoonfuls into the hot oil and, using the back of a spoon, flatten mixture slightly. Fry until golden brown on both sides, about 1 to 2 minutes per side. Drain on paper towels and serve immediately.

SERVES 4 TO 6 AS AN APPETIZER

Craig's Truffle Risotto

I had a few mouthfuls of heaven once at Butterfield 81, Ken Aretsky's cozy little Upper East Side restaurant in New York City. The chef there, Craig Cupani, was kind enough to share his recipe for truffle risotto with me, and even kinder to allow me to share it with you. Though it is one of the simplest risottos I've ever made, it is the perfect vehicle to highlight the delicate yet pungent flavor of this earthly treasure. Unlike most risottos, which are made with Arborio rice, this recipe calls for Carnaroli rice. It seems to produce a less sticky risotto, with rice grains remaining firm and separate. Carnaroli rice is a bit difficult to find in supermarkets, but can usually be found in gourmet markets, especially those that carry a wide array of Italian products. If you cannot find it, simply substitute Arborio. Truffle butter, truffles, and truffle- or basil-infused olive oil can be found at most upscale gourmet markets. I've had good results using truffles that come in small glass jars, and suggest a combination of white and black truffles. The white truffles definitely have a distinct, more pronounced truffle flavor.

6 cups chicken stock (or 6 cups water plus 3 chicken
    bouillon cubes)
1 large onion, finely chopped
4 tablespoons butter
1½ cups Italian Carnaroli rice
½ cup dry white wine
4 ounces truffle butter
⅓ cup heavy cream
¼ cup finely grated Parmigiano-Reggiano cheese
Salt and freshly ground black pepper, to taste
2 jars (.54 ounces each) preserved truffles (a combination of
    white and black, if available), finely shaven or sliced and
    juice reserved
⅔ cup truffle- or basil-infused olive oil, for garnish

In a medium saucepan, bring chicken stock to a low simmer.
In a large, heavy saucepan, sauté the onion in the butter over

medium heat until tender, about 5 minutes. Add the Carnaroli rice and cook 1 to 2 minutes, stirring constantly, until the rice is opaque. Do not allow the rice to brown.

Increase heat to medium-high and add the white wine. Cook, stirring constantly, until the rice has absorbed all the liquid.

Add ½ cup of the chicken stock to the rice. While stirring constantly, continue to add the remaining stock in ½-cup increments as the rice absorbs the liquid. Continue this until the rice is tender, usually 15 to 20 minutes. You may not need all of the stock. Add the truffle butter, any reserved juices from the jars of truffles, the heavy cream, and grated cheese and stir well to mix. Add salt and pepper.

Serve immediately, garnished with the shaved truffles and a tablespoon or two of truffle or basil olive oil.

SERVES 4 TO 6 AS AN APPETIZER

Grilled Vegetable Napoleons with Basil Vinaigrette

Taking part of its name from the classic stacked puff-pastry-and-custard napoleon, this napoleon's layers are comprised of tender grilled vegetables and an herbed goat cheese mixture. To tie it all together and make it just a bit more interesting, I've added a smooth basil and olive oil purée that has just a touch of vinegar—enough to call it a vinaigrette and to give the sweet vegetables and savory goat cheese a little kick.

Filling

6 ounces mild goat cheese, such as Montrachet
1½ tablespoons extra-virgin olive oil
4½ tablespoons sour cream
1 large clove garlic, pressed or minced
2 scallions, finely chopped
Salt and freshly ground black pepper, to taste

Vinaigrette

1 large clove garlic, pressed or minced
2 tablespoons balsamic vinegar
1 teaspoon salt
Scant 1 cup fresh basil leaves
1 cup extra-virgin olive oil

1 medium eggplant, cut crosswise into ¼-inch slices
1 medium or 2 small zucchini, cut lengthwise into ¼-inch slices
1 medium or 2 small yellow squash, cut lengthwise into
    ¼-inch slices
1 red onion, cut crosswise into ¼-inch slices
3 bell peppers, preferably 1 each green, red, and yellow,
    roasted (see roasting procedure page 90), quartered
Fresh basil leaves, for garnish
½ cup coarsely chopped pitted Kalamata olives, for garnish

Combine all the ingredients for the filling in a small bowl and stir well to mix. Cover with plastic wrap and set aside at room temperature until ready to assemble the napoleons.

Combine the garlic, vinegar, salt and basil leaves in a blender and process, adding the oil in a thin stream until the sauce is smooth and emulsified. Set aside, covered, in a nonreactive bowl or pitcher until ready to serve the napoleons.

Place the eggplant slices in a colander or lay flat on paper towels and sprinkle with salt. Let stand at least 30 minutes, turning once during the procedure and sprinkling the other side with salt. Do the same with the zucchini and yellow squash slices.

Meanwhile, prepare a fire in the grill.

Brush the eggplant, zucchini, yellow squash, and red onion slices with olive oil and grill over medium-hot coals until they soften and acquire grill marks, about 2 to 3 minutes. Turn the vegetables over and repeat on the other side. Season with salt and pepper to taste.

Assemble the napoleons: Layer the vegetables and goat cheese in individual stacks starting with 1 piece of zucchini, then followed by 1 piece of yellow squash, 1 to 2 teaspoons of the goat cheese filling, 1 piece of eggplant, another dollop of the goat cheese filling, 1 piece of each of the roasted peppers, and finally 1 slice red onion.

The napoleons can be served either warm or at room temperature. The microwave is a great way to heat individual napoleons after they've been assembled. Otherwise, place them on a lightly greased baking sheet and heat in a warm (250°F) oven, lightly covered with aluminum foil. Before serving, drizzle each napoleon with about 3 tablespoons of the basil vinaigrette, and garnish with fresh basil leaves and Kalamata olives, if desired.

SERVES 4 TO 6

NOTE: If you are concerned about fat calories, do what I often do: "grill" vegetables on top of the stove in a nonstick skillet. Simply get the skillet very hot and cook the vegetables, each in a single layer, with only salt and pepper. No oil is needed. As you finish cooking each type of vegetable, stack in a baking dish and keep covered with foil or plastic wrap.

Simmering Soups

Black Bean Soup with Fresh Tomato Salsa
White Bean and Tomato Soup
Black-Eyed Pea Soup
Gingered Carrot Soup
Colombian Chicken Soup
Chickpea Soup with Fresh Rosemary
Southern Corn Chowder
Escarole Soup
Pan-Roasted Garlic Soup
Lamb Soup with Zucchini and Tomato
Oxtail Soup with Winter Vegetables
Oyster Stew
Potato and Andouille Sausage Soup
Chunky Cream of Tomato Soup
Summer Tomato Soup with Fresh Basil Purée

Black Bean Soup with Fresh Tomato Salsa

I don't know one person who doesn't like black bean soup. This recipe is sure to be a crowd-pleaser, and can be made quickly with canned beans if you're short on time. You can alter the amount of crushed red pepper and jalapeño pepper if you're catering to timid palates, but be sure to make the Fresh Tomato Salsa. It's the perfect way to garnish the soup.

¼ cup olive oil
2 large onions, finely chopped
1 medium rib celery, finely chopped
6 cloves garlic, pressed or minced
1 medium red bell pepper, seeded and coarsely chopped
2 teaspoons ground cumin
1 teaspoon chili powder
1 teaspoon dried oregano
12 ounces dried black beans, cooked according to package directions until tender, or 3 cans (15 ounces each) of black beans, undrained
3 cups water
½ teaspoon crushed red pepper
1½ teaspoons Tabasco jalapeño sauce or
    1 jalapeño pepper, seeded and finely chopped
    (wear gloves please!)
¼ cup chopped fresh cilantro
Salt and freshly ground black pepper, to taste

Garnish
½ cup sour cream
Fresh Tomato Salsa (recipe follows)
Chopped fresh cilantro

In a large, heavy saucepan, heat the oil over medium heat. Add the onion, celery, garlic, and bell pepper and sauté until tender, about 5 minutes. Add the cumin, chili powder, and oregano and cook, stirring, another 1 to 2 minutes to wake up the spices. Add the beans and their cooking (or canning) liquid all at once, stirring well. Add the water and crushed red pepper and stir well. Lower the heat and simmer the mixture, uncovered, for 15 minutes, stirring occasionally.

After the soup has cooked for 15 minutes, add the Tabasco or jalapeño pepper and simmer uncovered another 20 minutes, or until the soup reaches the desired thickness. Add the cilantro and salt and pepper.

Garnish each serving with a dollop of sour cream, a spoonful of salsa, and a little chopped cilantro.

SERVES 6

Fresh Tomato Salsa

This is only to be made with the ripest, most beautiful in-season tomatoes you can find. It is a must with the preceding Black Bean Soup as well as Colombian Chicken Soup (page 26), and can make an otherwise uneventful dish something special. It is excellent over sautéed red snapper, Red Beans and Rice (see page 75), or even on an impromptu sandwich if you happen to find a leftover chicken breast in your fridge.

> 3 very ripe fresh tomatoes, halved, seeded, and finely
>   chopped
> 2 scallions, finely chopped
> 2 cloves garlic, crushed and mashed into a paste with
>   ½ teaspoon fine sea salt
> Juice of 1 lime or lemon
> 2 jalapeño peppers, seeded and very finely minced
>   (wear gloves please!)
> ¼ cup finely chopped fresh cilantro
> Salt, to taste

Combine all the ingredients except the salt in a glass or stainless-steel bowl and mix well. Allow to stand 15 minutes to let the flavors develop. Season with salt.

MAKES ABOUT 1½ CUPS

NOTE: Basil can be substituted for the cilantro, giving the salsa a very different flavor.

White Bean and Tomato Soup

Unless you're in New Orleans, where red beans reign supreme, white beans rank right alongside black beans as comfort food for most people. This is a soup that can be made quickly, yet never fails to garner praise.

¼ cup olive oil
2 large onions, chopped
1 medium rib celery, finely chopped
4 cloves garlic, pressed or minced
½ medium red bell pepper, seeded and finely chopped
¼ teaspoon crushed red pepper
1 teaspoon herbes de Provence
2 cans (15 ounces each) white beans (cannellini), undrained
1 can (28 ounces) Italian plum tomatoes, coarsely chopped, undrained
2 cups chicken stock (or 2 cups water plus 1 chicken bouillon cube)
Salt and freshly ground black pepper, to taste

In a heavy medium saucepan, heat the oil over medium heat. Add the onions, celery, garlic, and bell pepper and sauté until tender, about 5 minutes. Add the crushed red pepper and herbes de Provence and sauté another 5 minutes. Add the beans with their juice and cook, uncovered, for 15 minutes. Add the tomatoes and chicken stock, and simmer another 30 minutes. Season with salt and pepper and serve.

SERVES 6

Black-Eyed Pea Soup

I was always happy when New Year's Day rolled around because I knew that along with the promise of health for the coming year, it was a sure thing that black-eyed peas would find their way to my plate. Whether this southern tradition finds its root in truth—as we do know how healthful peas and beans are—or in fiction, I am not sure. Perhaps a frustrated, impoverished mother could think of no other way to justify the starring role of peas on such a celebratory occasion! In any case, this soup is a good way to enjoy black-eyed peas any time of the year.

3 tablespoons olive oil or vegetable oil
2 large onions, chopped
1 medium rib celery, finely chopped
½ medium green bell pepper, seeded and chopped
5 cloves garlic, pressed or minced
1 smoked ham hock, skin slit in several places with a sharp
  knife, or 8 ounces smoked ham (see Note below)
4 medium carrots, peeled and coarsely grated
1 package (16 ounces) dried black-eyed peas, well rinsed and
  picked over
8 to 10 cups water
1 or 2 jalapeño peppers, seeded and finely minced
  (wear gloves please!)
Salt and freshly ground black pepper, to taste

In a large, heavy saucepan, heat the oil over medium heat. Add the onion, celery, bell pepper, and garlic and sauté until tender, about 5 minutes.

Add the ham hock and grated carrots and cook 5 minutes, or until the slits in the hock start to open. Add the drained peas, 8 cups of water, and jalapeño peppers and bring the soup to a boil. Skim off any froth or scum which rises to the surface, then reduce the heat to low, cover, and simmer the soup 1½ to 2 hours, uncovering occasionally to stir, until the peas are soft and start to fall apart.

Adjust the consistency, adding more water if the soup has become too thick, or, if too thin, continue to cook until the liquid has reduced the desired amount (see Note). Season with salt and pepper. This soup freezes remarkably well, but will always need to be thinned upon reheating.

SERVES 6 TO 8

NOTE: If you are using regular smoked ham, you can either leave it in one piece or cube it, depending on whether you want the ham just for flavoring or would actually like small pieces of it in the soup.

Another way of thickening the soup is to mash some of the peas against the inside of the pot with the back of a wooden spoon.

Gingered Carrot Soup

I like to serve this soup as a prelude to Garlic Roast Leg of Lamb with Rosemary (page 136), Short Ribs with Sweet Potatoes and Indian Spices (page 132), or Crab Cakes with Two Sauces (page 88).

3 tablespoons butter
2 medium onions, coarsely chopped
⅓ cup finely chopped fresh ginger
2 cloves garlic, pressed or minced
3 pounds carrots, peeled, and cut into 1-inch pieces
8 cups chicken stock (or 8 cups water plus 2 chicken bouillon cubes), plus more as needed
¼ teaspoon cayenne pepper
½ cup heavy cream
Salt, to taste
Sweet paprika or cayenne pepper, or crème fraîche and snipped fresh chives, for garnish

In a heavy medium saucepan, melt the butter over medium-low heat. Add the onions, ginger, and garlic and sauté until tender, about 6 minutes. Add the carrots and 6 cups of the stock, increase the heat to high, and bring to a boil. Add the cayenne pepper, then cover saucepan and reduce the heat to low. Simmer for 45 minutes to 1 hour, or until the carrots are very tender.

Remove from the heat. Purée the soup, in batches, in a blender until very smooth, adding extra stock or water as necessary to aid in puréeing. Return the soup to a clean pot and add the heavy cream and stock or water to correct the consistency of the soup, if necessary. The soup should be thick enough to coat the back of a wooden spoon. Add salt and reheat the soup over gentle heat. Serve garnished with a pinch of paprika or cayenne pepper, or a dollop of crème fraîche and a sprinkling of snipped chives.

SERVES 8

Colombian Chicken Soup

If you love homemade chicken soup, like most of us do, I promise you that this version will leave you speechless. At first it seemed a strange concept to me, putting lime juice in my chicken soup, but my Colombian friend Luz has shown me the light. Typically, this soup is a one-dish meal, served with hot *arrepas* as an accompaniment (*arrepas* are small Colombian cornbreads that can be found in certain Spanish markets). If you can't find *arrepas*, regular cornbread may be substituted.

Stock

1 chicken (3½ to 4 pounds), skinned and cut into 8 pieces,
    plus 1 whole chicken breast, skinned and cut in half
1 medium onion, quartered
2 medium carrots, cut into 4 pieces
1 medium rib celery, cut into 4 pieces
1 bay leaf
3 cloves garlic, pressed or minced
½ bunch fresh cilantro, stems only (leaves reserved for soup)

Soup

1 medium onion, finely chopped
3 medium carrots, peeled and finely chopped
1 medium rib celery, finely chopped
5 baking potatoes (about 2 pounds), peeled and cut into
    ½-inch cubes
Juice of 1 lemon or lime
2 cloves garlic, pressed or minced
½ bunch cilantro, leaves only, finely chopped
2 scallions, finely chopped
½ chicken bouillon cube or 1 teaspoon chicken base
3 tablespoons olive oil

¼ teaspoon Bijol (available at Spanish food markets) or a
pinch each ground cumin and saffron threads

Fresh Tomato Salsa (page 21)

Combine all the ingredients for the stock in a large soup pot
and cover with cold water. Bring to a boil over high heat, then reduce the heat to low and simmer, uncovered, for 1½ to 2 hours,
skimming the scum off the top as it simmers, until the chicken
pulls away from the bone. Add water as necessary to keep the stock
ingredients covered.

Strain the stock through a coarse sieve, discarding everything except the boiled chicken, and return the stock to the rinsed-
out pot. Remove the chicken from the bones and shred into small
pieces. Set aside.

Add the onion, carrots, celery, and potatoes to the stock and
simmer 20 to 30 minutes, or until the potatoes are tender.

While the soup is simmering, combine the lemon or lime
juice, garlic, cilantro leaves, scallions, bouillon cube, oil, and Bijol
in a small bowl and mash into a paste with a fork.

When the potatoes are tender, add the reserved chicken and
seasoning paste to the soup and stir well to combine. Allow the
soup to return to a simmer, then remove from the heat and let sit,
covered, 10 minutes before serving. Serve garnished with a teaspoon of the salsa.

SERVES 6 TO 8 AS A FIRST COURSE

Chickpea Soup with Fresh Rosemary

My first brush with chickpeas came when I was eight years old. A neighbor introduced my mom to a salad made with chickpeas and other mixed vegetables. The chickpeas seemed quite foreign to us at the time, but being bean lovers already, they found a natural home on our table. Since then, they have become almost indispensable in my kitchen—they're wonderful in salads, they make a great dip, and they add something special to an otherwise uneventful lamb or chicken stew. They are incredibly versatile, and I suppose this could be the reason you can find them in almost every international cuisine. They go by a variety of names: chickpeas, garbanzo beans, ceci. And they do look like the tiniest little chickens, don't they? This soup can be a wonderfully substantial meal when served with a loaf of hot, crusty French or Italian bread.

2 large onions, chopped
1 medium rib celery, thinly sliced on the diagonal
4 large cloves garlic, pressed or minced
3 tablespoons olive oil, plus additional for serving, if desired
½ teaspoon crushed red pepper
2 cans (15½ ounces each) chickpeas, drained of half their liquid
6 cups chicken stock (or 6 cups water plus 3 chicken bouillon cubes)
1 tablespoon chopped fresh rosemary
Salt and freshly ground black pepper, to taste
2 to 3 tablespoons heavy cream
½ cup finely grated Parmigiano-Reggiano cheese, for garnish (optional)

In a large, heavy saucepan, heat the oil over medium heat. Add the onion, celery, and garlic and sauté until tender, about 5 minutes. Add the crushed red pepper and continue to cook, stirring constantly, for 1 or 2 minutes. Add the partially drained chickpeas, chicken stock, and rosemary and bring to a boil. Reduce the heat to low and simmer the soup for at least 45 minutes, stirring occasionally, until the chickpeas begin to fall apart and the soup thickens slightly. If the soup becomes too thick, thin with a little water. Season with salt and pepper.

Just before serving, stir in the heavy cream. Ladle into soup bowls and garnish, if desired, with grated cheese and a drizzle of olive oil.

SERVES 6 AS A FIRST COURSE

Southern Corn Chowder

Lots of variations of corn soup are found in the south, and this is my version. I have added potatoes to make it a hearty, filling soup that can be served as an opening to a special meal or as a meal in itself. Although it is best made with fresh corn at its peak, when kernels are sweet and tender, I have also had good results with frozen sweet corn.

Sometimes just for naughtiness's sake, I'll throw in a minced fresh jalapeño pepper if I have one on hand. This should be added when you whisk in the stock. And remember, use caution, as peppers can very greatly in heat potential. A general rule to follow is that the more mature a pepper is, the hotter. Mature peppers tend to be darker green and sometimes look a little worn.

This soup can be made in advance, as it freezes well. Take care to re-heat slowly over low heat, stirring frequently, to avoid scorching the soup.

4 ounces bacon, sliced
1 large onion, chopped
½ medium red bell pepper, seeded and chopped
1 medium rib celery, finely chopped
2 cloves garlic, pressed or minced
3 tablespoons all-purpose flour
8 cups chicken stock (or 8 cups water plus 3 chicken
   bouillon cubes)
1 large baking potato, peeled and cut into ½-inch cubes
2 sprigs fresh thyme or ¼ teaspoon dried
½ teaspoon crushed red pepper
4 cups fresh corn kernels (about 8 ears) or 2 packages
   (12 ounces each) frozen corn kernels
1 cup heavy cream
½ cup chopped scallions
Salt and cayenne pepper, to taste

In a large saucepan over high heat, cook the bacon until crisp. Remove to paper towels to drain.

Discard all but ¼ cup of the bacon fat from the saucepan, and in it sauté the onion, bell pepper, and celery over high heat until tender, about 5 minutes. Add the garlic and continue to cook another 1 to 2 minutes, stirring constantly so the garlic doesn't scorch.

Add the flour and cook 1 to 2 minutes, stirring constantly. Do not let the flour take on any color—if this starts to happen, reduce the heat immediately. After the flour has cooked 2 minutes, whisk in the stock and bring to a boil. Add the potato, thyme, and crushed red pepper. Skim any froth or scum from the top of the soup and reduce the heat so that the soup just simmers. Cook, covered, for 15 to 20 minutes, until the potatoes are just tender.

Stir in the corn, heavy cream, and scallions. Cook another 10 minutes or so, until the corn is tender.

Remove 1 cup of the soup from the pot and purée in a blender or food processor until very smooth. Return the puréed soup to the pot, stir well, and season with salt and pepper. Serve garnished with the reserved bacon, crumbled.

SERVES 6 TO 8 AS A FIRST COURSE

Escarole Soup

I don't think I even knew what escarole was until I moved to New York and started eating in Italian restaurants, but being a big fan of greens of all sorts, it was instant appreciation. I love its bitterness, but that is the precise quality that sometimes bothers others. The long, slow simmering of this soup mellows out the usually strong flavor, leaving tender greens. This is a soup that makes you feel like you're eating something good for you.

¼ cup olive oil
1 large onion, chopped
10 cloves garlic, pressed or minced
2 large heads escarole, cleaned and tough ribs removed, cut into rough strips or chopped
¼ teaspoon crushed red pepper
8 cups chicken stock (or 8 cups water plus 2 chicken bouillon cubes)
Salt and freshly ground black pepper, to taste
1 cup finely grated Parmigiano-Reggiano cheese, for garnish (optional)

In a heavy medium saucepan, heat the oil over medium heat. Add the onion and sauté until tender, about 5 minutes. Add the garlic and crushed red pepper and cook 2 to 3 minutes, stirring constantly, so the garlic doesn't scorch.

Add the chicken stock and bring to a boil, skimming any froth or scum from the top of the soup. Reduce the heat to low and simmer the soup, uncovered, for 30 minutes, or until the garlic has mellowed.

Add the escarole and continue to simmer until the escarole is tender, usually 15 to 20 minutes. Season with salt and pepper. Serve topped with a heaping tablespoon of grated cheese, if desired.

SERVES 6 TO 8 AS A FIRST COURSE

Pan-Roasted Garlic Soup

Does garlic scare you? Are you one of those people who wince at the thought of ingesting any more than the tiniest bit of it? Well, get over it! Garlic is one of life's true treasures. Not only does it add depth and character to anything we choose to include it in, it also contains natural antibiotic properties that help us fight off infections and is reported to lower blood cholesterol levels if consumed on a regular basis. If you're already a garlic lover, you'll love this soup. If not, you'll be amazed at how sweet and mellow the garlic becomes after long, slow simmering.

20 cloves garlic, pressed or minced
¼ cup virgin or extra-virgin olive oil
2¾ quarts chicken stock (or 11 cups water plus 2 chicken
    bouillon cubes)
½ teaspoon crushed red pepper, or to taste
4 scallions, thinly sliced on the diagonal
¼ cup chopped fresh parsley
Salt and freshly ground black pepper, to taste

Garnish

6 ½-inch slices from a French baguette, toasted until golden
    and crisp-dry
6 tablespoons grated Parmigiano-Reggiano cheese
6 teaspoons extra-virgin olive oil

In a heavy 4-quart saucepan, heat the oil over low heat. Add the garlic and sauté for 2 to 3 minutes, until soft. Take care not to scorch the garlic, as this will produce a bitter flavor.

Add the chicken stock and crushed red pepper, increase the heat, and bring to a boil. Reduce the heat to low and simmer, uncovered, for at least 45 minutes. If at the end of simmering too much liquid has evaporated, add enough water to bring the level up to at least 8 cups. Add the scallions and parsley and continue to simmer until scallions have wilted, about 2 minutes. Season with salt and pepper and remove from the heat.

Ladle the soup into 6 bowls and top each serving with a slice of toasted French baguette. Sprinkle 1 tablespoon of cheese and drizzle 1 teaspoon of olive oil over the toast and soup in each bowl.

SERVES 6 AS A FIRST COURSE

NOTE: This soup can be amended to accompany a Latin-flavored meal simply by replacing the parsley with cilantro and omitting the bread and Parmesan. Finish instead with 1 egg yolk, stirring it into the soup after removing from the heat, just before serving.

Lamb Soup with Zucchini and Tomato

When I first moved to New York City, I worked the night shift at a restaurant called Serendipity III—not as a cook, but rather as a cashier. I had been pounding the pavement looking for a job when I walked by and saw a sign advertising a position available in their kitchen. The general manager took one look at me, rather petite and not at all imposing in demeanor, and tried to tell me in as nice a way as possible that she didn't think I was cut out for kitchen work, but that they could fit me in behind the cash register.

Having been in New York for over ten years now, I'm just a little bit tougher than I was when I first arrived, all dainty and southern-like, and can now sling pans at least a third of my size. However, I do consider my experience at Serendipity to be among the most formative and nurturing times of my life. I was dubbed "Casherella, Queen of Coins" and "Miss Breck" (I have lots of hair), two titles I am still most proud of. Owners Calvin Holt and Stephen Bruce took me under their wing, and I felt I had a sort of instant family in New York City. There is something magical about Serendipity, and I consider it serendipitous indeed that I began my life in New York there. I loved the fun food and the exciting atmosphere and would sometimes be inspired to go home and cook at three A.M. One night I went home and made this soup.

3 tablespoons canola or olive oil
2 pounds boneless lamb stew meat, such as shoulder or neck, cubed
1 large onion, chopped
1 medium rib celery, chopped
½ medium green bell pepper, seeded and chopped
4 cloves garlic, pressed or minced
2 sprigs fresh rosemary or 1 teaspoon dried, crumbled
¼ teaspoon crushed red pepper
1 35-ounce can Italian plum tomatoes, undrained and broken up with your hands
1 teaspoon dried basil, crumbled

6 cups water
2 medium zucchini, quartered lengthwise, then cut
    crosswise into ¼-inch pieces
Salt and freshly ground black pepper, to taste
¼ cup finely grated Parmigiano-Reggiano cheese, for
    garnish (optional)

In a heavy medium saucepan, heat the oil over high heat. When almost smoking, add the lamb and brown well on all sides. Reduce the heat to medium and add the onion, celery, bell pepper, garlic, rosemary, and crushed red pepper. Cook until the vegetables are tender, about 5 minutes, stirring constantly to avoid scorching.

Add the tomatoes, basil, and water, mixing well. Increase the heat to high and bring the soup to a boil, skimming any froth or scum from the top. Cover and reduce the heat so the soup just simmers. Cook for 1 to 1½ hours, uncovering occasionally to stir, until the meat is very tender and its flavor has permeated the soup.

Add the zucchini and cook until very tender, usually 20 minutes or so. Season with salt and pepper and remove from the heat.

Serve sprinkled with the grated cheese, if desired.

SERVES 6 AS A FIRST COURSE

Oxtail Soup with Winter Vegetables

After getting over my initial dismay over the name of this particular cut of beef, I gave way to my more basic feelings of curiosity and intrigue. We'd never had oxtails at home, and I had absolutely no idea what they were. So, I set about researching, and I learned that, like shanks, this cut of meat lends itself well to any sort of braising, creating a very rich, thick stock because of the amount of gelatin it contains. Oxtails are thus particularly suitable to soups and stews.

The recipe that follows is a nice version of a basic oxtail soup. The orange juice and zest, along with the sweetness of the potatoes, serve to take the edge off the strong beef flavor. So, if you're looking for the heartiest of hearty soups, something to warm you up in the dead of winter, try this recipe. But be warned: Oxtails cannot be rushed. This soup takes time, and will always taste better if eaten the day after it was prepared or after having been frozen. It may be easily transformed into a stew by simply adding less water, and is wonderful over white rice or couscous.

¼ cup canola oil
4 pounds oxtails
1 large onion
2 medium ribs celery
¼ cup chopped green bell pepper
8 large cloves garlic, pressed or minced
3 tablespoons red wine vinegar
2½ to 3 quarts water
3 tablespoons tomato paste
1 cup freshly squeezed orange juice
3 teaspoons grated orange zest
4 carrots, peeled and cut into ½-inch slices
4 parsnips, peeled and cut into ½-inch slices
1 large sweet potato, peeled and cut into ¾-inch cubes
2 purple-topped turnips, peeled and cut into ¾-inch cubes
Salt and freshly ground black pepper, to taste
Chopped fresh cilantro, for garnish

In a large, heavy saucepan, heat the oil over high heat until it is hot and almost smoking. Add the oxtails and brown well on all sides. Using a slotted spoon, remove the oxtails to a bowl and set aside.

Add the onion, celery, and bell pepper to the saucepan and sauté over high heat, until the vegetables are tender and begin to caramelize around the edges, about 5 to 7 minutes, stirring frequently. Add the garlic and cook 1 to 2 minutes, stirring constantly so the garlic doesn't scorch. Add the vinegar and stir to loosen any browned bits sticking to the bottom of the pan.

Add 2 quarts of the water, the tomato paste, orange juice, orange zest, and reserved oxtails to the pan and stir well to mix. Bring the soup to a boil and skim any froth or scum from the surface of the liquid. Cover and reduce the heat so the liquid just simmers.

Cook the oxtails 2½ to 3 hours, until almost tender, uncovering occasionally to stir and adding water if the soup seems too thick. Skim off any fat that rises to the surface.

When the oxtails are tender, add the carrots, parsnips, sweet potato, and turnips and simmer, uncovered, until vegetables are tender, about 20 minutes.

Adjust consistency by adding water if the soup has become too thick. Season with salt and pepper and serve garnished with chopped cilantro.

SERVES 8 AS A FIRST COURSE

Oyster Stew

I have a crisp memory of my first oyster, ingested at age three. PaPa LaChute used to open sacks of oysters in front of his house on the River Road. My mom would stand and talk with PaPa while he dug around in the sack for her favorite oysters, the very tiniest ones. This was their time alone together, and I knew from watching that this was very serious, this oyster business, with so much closeness passing between my mom and her daddy. When one day they suggested that I might like to try one, I secretly had my doubts—but didn't for a second consider not going through with it. PaPa was laughing, I remember, and mom just kept saying, "Isn't it good, Charlotte? Mmmm, good." What could I say? It was definitely intriguing, a most unusual sensation, but I so wanted to be part of their ritual that I told myself, yes, this is good. Today there are no questions in my mind about oysters. I love them however they are prepared.

This is one of the best, and simplest, ways to eat them—a very traditional version of a classic.

7 tablespoons butter
1 medium onion, finely chopped
4 tablespoons all-purpose flour
2½ dozen oysters, shucked, with their liquor
1 cup heavy cream
4 cups milk
1 bunch scallions, green tops only, thinly sliced
Salt and freshly ground black pepper, to taste
Oyster crackers, for serving (optional)

In a large, heavy saucepan, melt 4 tablespoons of the butter over medium-low heat. Add the onion and sauté until it is tender, 5 to 6 minutes. Do not allow the onion to brown. Stir in the flour and cook 1 to 2 minutes, stirring constantly. Do not allow the flour to brown. Strain oyster liquor from the oysters and add it to the saucepan, along with the cream and milk. Whisk well to mix and allow to simmer, uncovered, 20 minutes or until thickened, stirring occasionally.

Add the scallion tops to the saucepan and let simmer 10 minutes. Add the oysters and cook another 5 to 10 minutes, until oysters are just cooked through. (Overcooking will result in tough, chewy oysters.) Remove from the heat and season with salt and pepper. Add the remaining 3 tablespoons butter to the soup (it will float on top). Serve with oyster crackers if desired.

SERVES 6 AS A FIRST COURSE

Potato and Andouille Sausage Soup

This is a soup for a brave soul on a cold winter's day. Because of the Cajun *andouille* sausage it is warming in more ways than one, though not overpoweringly so. You should be able to find *andouille* in any gourmet supermarket, but if you have trouble procuring some, try your butcher. With a little notice, butchers are often able to obtain items they do not normally keep in stock. You could also substitute Moroccan *merguez* or Mexican *chorizo*, two different sausages that are spicy in similar ways, with different but good results.

2 tablespoons olive oil
8 ounces *andouille* sausage, removed from its casings and
    broken into bite-size pieces
1 large onion, chopped
1 medium leek, white and light green parts only, cleaned
    well, and thinly sliced
½ medium red bell pepper, seeded and finely chopped
4 cloves garlic, pressed or minced
1 teaspoon dried thyme, crumbled
¼ teaspoon dried marjoram, crumbled
2½ pounds Yukon Gold potatoes, peeled and cut into
    ½-inch cubes
2½ quarts chicken stock (or 10 cups water plus 3 chicken
    bouillon cubes)
1 bay leaf
1 jalapeño pepper, seeded and minced (wear gloves please!)
¼ cup heavy cream
½ teaspoon Worcestershire sauce
½ teaspoon Tony Chachere's Creole Seasoning
Salt and cayenne pepper, to taste
¼ cup chopped fresh parsley, for garnish

In a large, heavy saucepan, heat the oil over medium-high heat. Add the sausage and brown well on all sides. Add the onion,

leek, bell pepper, and garlic and sauté until tender, about 5 minutes. Add the thyme, marjoram, potatoes, chicken stock, bay leaf,
and jalapeño pepper and bring the soup to a boil. Skim off any
froth or scum from the top of the soup and reduce the heat so the
soup just simmers. Cook 30 to 40 minutes, until the potatoes are
tender.

Stir in the heavy cream, Worcestershire sauce, and seasoned
salt and remove from the heat. Season with salt and cayenne pepper. Remove the bay leaf before serving, garnished with the
chopped parsley.

SERVES 8 TO 10 AS A FIRST COURSE

Chunky Cream of Tomato Soup

Not at all your typical tomato soup, this is loaded with chunky vegetables and tomatoes, all in a slightly-creamy-but-not-sinfully-so tomato base. Simple basil is my favorite flavor enhancer here, and if fresh basil is available, this is best. Do remember that fresh basil should be chopped at the last minute so it won't discolor. For a slightly different taste, if you are especially fond of herbes de Provence, you can substitute the same amount of this for dried basil.

3 tablespoons butter
2 large onions, chopped
2 medium ribs celery, chopped
6 cloves garlic, pressed or minced
3 tablespoons all-purpose flour
2 cans (28 ounces each) Italian plum tomatoes, undrained
    and coarsely chopped
¼ cup chopped fresh basil or 1 teaspoon dried
¼ teaspoon crushed red pepper
1¾ to 2 cups water
1 chicken bouillon cube
½ cup heavy cream
Salt and freshly ground black pepper, to taste
½ teaspoon sugar, if needed
Chopped fresh basil, for garnish (optional)

In an enameled or other nonreactive medium saucepan, melt the butter over medium heat. Add the onions, celery, and garlic and sauté until tender, about 5 minutes. Add the flour and cook another minute, stirring constantly. Add the tomatoes, basil, crushed red pepper, 1½ cups water, and chicken bouillon cube and simmer 30 minutes, stirring frequently.

Add the heavy cream and cook 10 minutes longer, then remove from the heat. This soup should be thick, but if it is too thick for your taste, add ¼ to ½ cup of water to correct the consistency. Season with salt and pepper and, if the soup tastes too acidic, add the sugar.

Serve the soup garnished with chopped fresh basil, if desired.

SERVES 6 AS A FIRST COURSE

Summer Tomato Soup
with Fresh Basil Purée

This is a wonderful soup to make in late summer when there is no shortage of plump, ripe tomatoes. Don't attempt it with fresh tomatoes in winter or with those things they call tomatoes in the supermarket which are colorless, tasteless, waxy things for people who know no better. Instead, substitute canned Italian plum tomatoes. This soup is delicious hot or cold—just remember that anything seasoned while hot will need more seasoning if you opt to serve it cold. The fresh basil purée is essential to this soup.

¾ cup olive oil
2 large onions, coarsely chopped
6 cloves garlic, pressed or minced
2 medium ribs celery, finely chopped
¼ teaspoon crushed red pepper
4 pounds fresh, ripe tomatoes, roughly chopped, or 2 cans
    (28 ounces each) Italian plum tomatoes, undrained and
    broken up with your hands
1 cup water, plus more if needed for puréeing
2 cups (firmly packed) fresh basil leaves, rinsed and
    patted dry
2 teaspoons sugar, if needed
Salt and freshly ground black pepper, to taste

In a medium enameled or other nonreactive saucepan, heat ¼ cup of the oil over medium heat. Add the onion, 4 cloves of the garlic, and the celery and sauté until tender, 5 to 7 minutes, stirring occasionally. Add the crushed red pepper and tomatoes and continue to cook, covered, until the tomatoes give up their liquid and begin to fall apart, about 15 minutes. If you are using fresh tomatoes, add 1 cup water at this point and continue to cook, covered, until the tomatoes have completely broken up, another 15 minutes (see Note).

While the soup is cooking, combine the basil leaves, remaining 2 cloves garlic, and remaining ½ cup oil in a blender and process until smooth. Season with salt and pepper and set aside, covered with plastic wrap, until ready to use (see Note).

Remove the soup from the heat and purée, in batches, in a blender. Strain it through a fine-meshed sieve, discarding the solids. If serving the soup hot, pour it into a clean saucepan and keep warm until serving. If serving it cold, pour it into a heatproof bowl and let cool to room temperature, then chill in the refrigerator for at least 2 hours. Just before serving, season with salt and pepper and, if the tomatoes seem overly acidic, add sugar as necessary.

Serve the soup in bowls, garnished with dollops of the fresh basil purée.

SERVES 6

NOTE: If you are using canned tomatoes, add the cup of water along with the tomatoes and simmer 30 minutes.

The basil purée can be made up to 1 day in advance and refrigerated, covered. Let it return to room temperature before using.

Pasta Presto

Though the pasta I grew up with was simple, requisite stuff (MaMa LaChute's spaghetti gravy, Mom's meat sauce, stuffed shells, and, of course, macaroni and cheese), I was happily introduced to the myriad of possibilities pasta affords when I moved to New York, home to so many remarkable Italian restaurants. I was intrigued by some of the unusual sauces and toppings I found there, and was ecstatic to learn of all the different shapes of pasta available. Pasta sauces, like soups, invite experimentation and are accepting of substitutions. They are another great way to clean out the fridge or pantry, and a great sauce can be made from relatively little: a good bottle of olive oil, a bit of garlic, and some freshly grated Parmesan cheese is one of the simplest and yet most delicious ways to enjoy pasta. Try adding fresh herbs or reconstituted dried mushrooms and you have something altogether different. One of my favorite "instant" sauces is a bit of olive paste, olive oil and freshly grated Parmesan cheese. (You can find olive paste in the specialty foods sections of many supermarkets, Italian grocery stores, or specialty food shops.)

One of the unifying elements of these pasta recipes is the use of Parmigiano-Reggiano cheese. If you are not already familiar with Parmigiano-Reggiano's unparalleled superior nature among Parmesans, then I urge you to search it out. It can be found in the specialty cheese section of most supermarkets these days (its name is stamped on the rind), and should be bought in chunks, not already grated. Grating your own as needed allows the cheese to retain its natural moisture, and you will find that the taste and texture of freshly grated Parmigiano-Reggiano is like nothing else. You should make sure to have it on hand when its flavor is highlighted, as when it is grated on top of prepared pasta. Another

Parmesan of exceptional quality that comes from Italy and is less known (hence less expensive) is Grana Padano. It is a more than acceptable substitute for Parmigiano-Reggiano if you happen to come across it.

The recipes that follow combine my favorite sauces with various types of pasta that I have found work best together. Please keep in mind, these are only suggested combinations and each can be tailored to suit your taste. If you'd like to substitute rigatoni for penne—by all means! Experiment and discover how much the character of a sauce can change just by pairing it with a different partner. It's part of the fun of cooking with pasta and what makes pasta possibilities endless.

Pastas

Cappellini with Fresh Plum Tomatoes and Basil
Cavatelli with Chickpea and Broccoli Sauce
Farfalle with Shrimp and Scallops in Saffron Cream Sauce
Fusilli with Smoked Salmon and Green Peas
Linguine with Braised Garlic, Balsamic Vinegar, and Fresh Herbs
Penne alla Puttanesca
Penne Rigate with Three Blue Cheeses
Rotelle with Pesto Cream Sauce and Sea Scallops
Spaghetti with Creamy Tomato and Italian Sausage Sauce
Vermicelli with Chicken Liver and Spicy Tomato Sauce

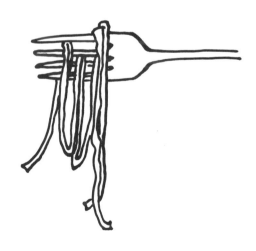

Cappellini with Fresh Plum Tomatoes and Basil

Here is a wonderfully light, delicious pasta sauce for summertime when ripe tomatoes are the only ones to be had. I like to make it with fresh plum tomatoes, riper than ripe, and I don't believe in peeling them, as so many of the tomato's nutrients are lost this way, not to mention it being a laborious process—why get rid of nature's roughage? I like to keep the sauce a bit on the brothy side and eat it in a big bowl, preferably with cappellini.

Sauce

¼ cup extra-virgin olive oil
1 large or 2 medium onions, roughly chopped
2 medium ribs celery, roughly chopped or sliced
8 cloves garlic, pressed or minced
5 pounds fresh plum tomatoes, chopped in 1-inch pieces
½ cup rich chicken stock (or ½ cup water plus 1½ chicken bouillon cubes)
½ teaspoon crushed red pepper
½ cup finely chopped fresh basil
Salt and freshly ground black pepper, to taste
1 teaspoon sugar, if needed

2 pounds dried cappellini (angel hair)
Fresh basil leaves, for garnish
½ cup freshly grated Parmigiano-Reggiano cheese, for serving

In a large enameled or other nonreactive skillet or low-sided sauté pan, heat the oil over medium-high heat. Add the onion and celery and sauté until softened and excess moisture has reduced, 5 to 6 minutes, stirring frequently. Add the garlic and continue to cook another minute, stirring constantly so the garlic doesn't scorch. Add the tomatoes, chicken stock, and crushed red pepper and continue to cook over medium-high heat until the tomatoes have given up their juices and begin to fall apart, 10 to 15 minutes.

Add the chopped basil, then remove from the heat. Season with salt and pepper and, if the tomatoes seem overly acidic, add sugar as necessary. If you prefer a smoother sauce, purée a portion of the sauce in a blender or food processor and return it to the skillet, stirring well.

In a kettle or large saucepan, bring 5 quarts salted water to a boil. Add the pasta and return to a boil, stirring occasionally. Cook, stirring occasionally, until pasta is al dente, about 2 minutes. Drain the pasta in a colander, then transfer to a large bowl and toss with half of the fresh tomato sauce. Serve with remaining sauce ladled on top and garnish with fresh basil. Pass the grated cheese at the table.

SERVES 6 TO 8

Cavatelli with Chickpea and Broccoli Sauce

Yet another classic Italian sauce that is easy to make and incredibly delicious. When you make it at home you have control over the amount of cheese and olive oil you use, which can be a good thing if you're counting calories. I think this sauce is best suited to a substantial, chewier pasta shape, such as cavatelli or orecchiete. Drizzle a bit of olive oil over the pasta and sauce before serving and pass freshly grated Parmigiano-Reggiano at the table.

Sauce

¼ cup extra-virgin olive oil
1 large or 2 medium onions, coarsely chopped
6 cloves garlic, pressed or minced
2 cans (15½ ounces each) chickpeas, undrained
1½ cups chicken stock (or 1½ cups water plus 1 chicken bouillon cube)
1 bunch fresh broccoli, trimmed of stems and cut into flowerets
¾ teaspoon crushed red pepper
½ teaspoon dried basil, crumbled
Water, if needed
Salt and freshly ground black pepper, to taste

1 pound dried cavatelli or orecchiete
½ cup extra-virgin olive oil, for garnish
½ cup finely grated Parmigiano-Reggiano cheese, for serving

In a large saucepan, heat the olive oil over medium-high heat. Add the onion and sauté until tender and just beginning to caramelize around the edges, 5 to 7 minutes. Add the garlic and cook another minute, stirring constantly so the garlic doesn't scorch. Add the chickpeas and their liquid, chicken stock, crushed red pepper, and dried basil and bring to a boil, then reduce the heat and simmer, uncovered, for 10 to 15 minutes, or until the liquid has reduced and the chickpeas have begun to fall apart, about 15 minutes. Add broccoli flowerets and cook until tender, about 10 minutes (see Note). The sauce should be somewhat brothy. If it has reduced too much, add a bit of water so it reaches the desired consistency. Remove from the heat and season with salt and pepper.

In a kettle or large saucepan, bring 5 quarts of salted water to a boil. Add the pasta and return to a boil, stirring occasionally. Cook, stirring occasionally, until the pasta is al dente, 12 to 15 minutes.

Drain the pasta in a colander, then transfer to a large bowl and toss with half of the sauce. Serve with remaining sauce ladled on top and drizzled with olive oil. Pass the grated cheese at the table.

SERVES 4 TO 6

NOTE: If you'd prefer the broccoli to remain crisp, reduce cooking time accordingly.

Farfalle with Shrimp and Scallops in Saffron Cream Sauce

Farfalle is a festive pasta to begin with, but with the addition of shrimp and scallops in a saffron-scented cream sauce, this is a truly elegant dish. A simple green salad or steamed asparagus with Basic Vinaigrette (page 198) and a loaf of hot, crusty French bread complete this picture nicely.

Sauce

1 lemon
1 pound medium shrimp, shelled and deveined, shells reserved
1 large onion, chopped
1 medium rib celery, chopped
Few sprigs fresh parsley
4 or 5 whole black peppercorns
2 cups water
6 tablespoons butter or olive oil
1 medium red bell pepper, seeded and finely chopped
2 cloves garlic, pressed or minced
3 tablespoons all-purpose flour
3 cups heavy cream
2 generous pinches finest-quality saffron threads
   (approximately .5 grams)
¼ teaspoon crushed red pepper
1 medium zucchini, quartered lengthwise and thinly sliced
   crosswise
3 scallions, thinly sliced on the diagonal
1 pound sea scallops, rinsed and patted dry
¼ cup minced fresh parsley
Salt and freshly ground black pepper, to taste

1 pound dried farfalle (bow-tie pasta)
1 small bunch fresh chives, finely chopped
⅔ cup finely grated Parmigiano-Reggiano cheese, for
   serving

Remove a strip of peel 1 inch wide from the lemon. Set the lemon aside for another use. Combine the strip of peel, the reserved shrimp shells, about one fourth of the onion, half the celery, the parsley, black peppercorns, and 2 cups of water in a medium saucepan. Bring to a boil, then reduce the heat to low and simmer, uncovered, 15 minutes. Strain the liquid through a fine sieve into a clean bowl, pressing on the solids to extract as much liquid as possible. Set the stock aside.

In a large saucepan, melt 3 tablespoons of the butter over medium heat. Add the remaining onion and celery, the garlic, and red bell pepper and sauté until tender, about 5 minutes. Add the flour and continue to cook, stirring well, for 1 to 2 minutes. Do not let the flour brown. Add the reserved shrimp stock, ¼ cup at a time, and whisk until smooth.

Add the heavy cream, saffron, and crushed red pepper and bring to a boil. Reduce the heat to low and simmer about 20 minutes, until the desired consistency is reached.

Stir in the zucchini, scallions, and shrimp and cook until the vegetables are tender and the shrimp are just cooked through, 5 to 7 minutes.

Meanwhile, heat the remaining 3 tablespoons butter in a large skillet or sauté pan over medium-high heat. Just as the butter begins to brown, add the scallops and quickly sauté, browning on both sides, 2 to 3 minutes per side. Remove from the heat and add the scallops to the shrimp mixture. Stir, then remove from the heat. Add the parsley and season with salt and pepper.

In a kettle or large saucepan, bring 5 quarts of salted water to a boil. Add the pasta and return to a boil, stirring occasionally. Cook, stirring occasionally, until the pasta is al dente, 10 to 12 minutes.

Drain the pasta in a colander, then transfer to a large bowl and toss with half of the sauce. Serve with remaining sauce ladled on top, garnished with the chives. Pass the grated cheese at the table.

SERVES 6

Fusilli with Smoked Salmon and Green Peas

The rich sauce in this recipe goes a long way. It is incredibly delicious, with bits of lemon peel and tiny green peas interrupting the smooth creaminess. I like to serve this with fusilli pasta, but linguine, farfalle, or fettuccine work well also.

Sauce

3 tablespoons butter
1 small onion, finely chopped
1 clove garlic, pressed or minced
3 tablespoons all-purpose flour
2 cups heavy cream
1 cup milk
1 cup chicken or fish stock (or 1 cup water plus 1 chicken or fish bouillon cube)
1 teaspoon finely grated lemon zest
4 scallions, green tops only, thinly sliced
5 ounces smoked salmon, sliced and then cut into thin strips
⅔ cup fresh or frozen green peas
¼ cup finely chopped fresh parsley
Salt and freshly ground black pepper, to taste

1 pound dried fusilli
3 tablespoons chopped fresh chives (or scallions finely minced), for garnish
Finely grated Parmigiano-Reggiano cheese, for serving

In a large, heavy saucepan, melt the butter over medium heat. Add the onion and garlic and sauté until tender, about 5 minutes. Add the flour and cook another 1 to 2 minutes, stirring constantly. Do not allow the flour to brown.

Whisk in the heavy cream and then the milk little by little, then add the stock. Bring the sauce to a boil, then reduce the heat so the sauce just simmers. Cook, uncovered, stirring occasionally, for 15 to 20 minutes, or until sauce has thickened and flavors have come together.

Add the scallions and cook another 5 minutes, or until wilted. Add the smoked salmon and peas and cook about 5 minutes, or until the peas are cooked through. Remove from the heat, stir in the parsley, and season with salt and pepper.

In a kettle or large saucepan, bring 5 quarts of salted water to a boil. Add the pasta and return to a boil, stirring occasionally. Cook, stirring occasionally, until the pasta is al dente, 9 to 11 minutes.

Drain the pasta in a colander, then transfer to a large bowl and toss with half of the sauce. Serve with remaining sauce ladled on top, garnished with chives or scallions. Pass the grated cheese at the table.

SERVES 4 TO 6

Linguine with Braised Garlic, Balsamic Vinegar, and Fresh Herbs

Yet another recipe for garlic advocates, this is a wonderfully simple pasta sauce that can be prepared quickly and inexpensively, using ingredients that most of us typically keep on hand. Delicious with a loaf of crusty French bread and a simple green salad.

1 pound dried linguine
¼ cup extra-virgin olive oil
10 cloves garlic, pressed or minced
¼ teaspoon crushed red pepper
Water, if needed
3 tablespoons butter
½ cup chopped fresh parsley
¼ cup chopped fresh basil
1¼ cups freshly grated Parmigiano-Reggiano cheese
3 tablespoons balsamic vinegar
Salt and freshly ground black pepper, to taste

In a kettle or large saucepan, bring 5 quarts of salted water to a boil. Add the linguine and return to a boil, stirring occasionally. Cook, stirring occasionally, until the pasta is al dente, 10 to 12 minutes.

While the pasta is cooking, heat the oil in a large, heavy skillet over low heat. Add the garlic and sauté until soft, 5 to 7 minutes. Stir frequently, taking care not to let the garlic scorch. If it begins to scorch, add a few tablespoons of water.

When the linguine is al dente, drain it in a colander. Immediately add it to the sautéed garlic in the skillet, along with the butter, parsley, basil, grated cheese, and vinegar. Toss well to mix and season with salt and pepper. Serve immediately.

SERVES 4 TO 6

Penne alla Puttanesca

This is my all-time favorite pasta sauce. Though you can find it on many restaurant menus, it is a great sauce to make at home, as it is quick and uncomplicated, uses ingredients many of us always have on hand, and fills the house with such a delicious, heady aroma that it makes us wonder why we ever want to eat out anyway. For it to be a real success you cannot skimp on the ingredients. As for olives, my favorite ones for this sauce are Greek Kalamata olives. They can usually be purchased by the pound at any upscale gourmet food store or Italian or Greek deli. Don't bother with the ones in the jars, as you can tell just by looking at their pale, washed-out color that they are inferior. Quality capers also make a big difference, as do anchovies. I like nonpareil capers (I prefer their tiny buds) and anchovies from Italy, packed in olive oil in small glass jars (the unused portion can be left in the jar for storage in the refrigerator, unlike those anchovies found in small tins).

Sauce

¼ cup extra-virgin olive oil

1 large or 2 medium onions, coarsely chopped

8 cloves garlic, pressed or minced

1 can (28 ounces) Italian plum tomatoes, roughly chopped
  or puréed

8 ounces Kalamata olives, pitted and halved

¼ cup imported nonpareil capers, drained and liquid
  reserved

5 anchovy fillets, finely chopped, or to taste

½ teaspoon crushed red pepper

½ cup chopped fresh basil or 1 teaspoon dried, plus
  additional fresh leaves for garnishing if available

½ teaspoon Tony Chachere's Creole Seasoning

Freshly ground black pepper, to taste

1 teaspoon sugar, if needed

1 pound dried penne rigate
⅔ cup freshly grated Parmigiano-Reggiano cheese, for
   serving

In a large enameled or other nonreactive saucepan or skillet, heat the oil over medium-high heat. Add the onion and sauté until tender and beginning to caramelize around the edges, about 6 to 8 minutes. Add the garlic and cook 1 to 2 minutes, stirring constantly so the garlic doesn't scorch. Add the tomatoes, olives, capers, anchovies, crushed red pepper, and basil and bring to a boil. Reduce the heat to low and simmer, uncovered, 15 to 20 minutes, stirring occasionally, until the sauce has thickened and the flavors have come together. Remove from the heat. Taste the sauce and season with creole seasoning and pepper, adding a teaspoon or two of the reserved caper liquid if the caper component is lacking. If the tomatoes are too acidic, add the sugar.

Bring 5 quarts of salted water to a boil in a kettle or large saucepan. Add the pasta and return to a low boil, stirring occasionally. Cook, stirring occasionally, until the pasta is al dente, about 10 to 12 minutes.

Drain the pasta in a colander, then toss with half of the sauce in a large bowl. Serve with remaining sauce ladled on top, garnished with fresh basil, if desired. Pass the grated cheese at the table.

SERVES 4

Penne Rigate with Three Blue Cheeses

Roquefort is perhaps my favorite cheese on its own, but combining it with Gorgonzola and Saga blue creates an unmistakably rich pasta sauce that makes you feel you are communing with the gods. If penne rigate is unavailable, try this with fusilli, although any type of pasta with nooks and crannies for this sauce to hide in will work fine. I think a simple green salad with Basic Vinaigrette (page 198) and a loaf of hot, crusty French bread are all that are needed with this to make one happy.

Sauce

3 tablespoons butter
3 shallots, finely minced
1 clove garlic, pressed or minced
3 tablespoons all-purpose flour
4 cups heavy cream
2 sprigs fresh thyme
½ teaspoon freshly ground black pepper, or to taste
2 scallions, thinly sliced
¼ cup finely chopped fresh parsley
¼ pound Gorgonzola dolce, rind removed and crumbled
¼ pound Roquefort, crumbled
¼ pound Saga blue, rind removed and crumbled
Salt, if needed
¾ cup coarsely chopped walnuts, toasted

2 pounds dried penne rigate or fusilli

In a heavy 2-quart saucepan melt the butter over medium heat. Add the shallots and garlic and sauté until tender, about 5 minutes. Add the flour and cook 2 to 3 minutes, stirring constantly. Do not allow the flour to brown. Whisk in the heavy cream. Bring to a boil, then reduce the heat to low. Add the fresh thyme and black pepper and cook, uncovered, until the mixture thickens enough to coat the back of a spoon, 15 to 20 minutes. Add scallions and parsley and cook another 5 minutes, until scallions are wilted. Add cheeses and stir well to combine as they melt. Taste the sauce and add salt if necessary (see Note). Stir in ½ cup of the toasted walnuts, and remove from the heat.

In a kettle or large saucepan, bring 5 quarts of salted water to a boil. Add the pasta and return to a boil, stirring occasionally. Cook, stirring occasionally, until the pasta is al dente, about 10 minutes.

Drain the pasta in a colander, then transfer to a large bowl and toss with half of the sauce. Serve with remaining sauce ladled on top, garnished with the remaining walnuts.

SERVES 8

NOTE: Often no additional salt is needed due to the saltiness of the Roquefort.

Rotelle with Pesto Cream Sauce and Sea Scallops

People go crazy over this sauce, with or without the scallops. If they only knew how easy it is—I take the opportunity to make it whenever I have extra pesto lying around. It's a sinfully rich and delicious pasta sauce, dressed up or down. When sautéing the scallops, it is important not to overcook them, as this will result in tough, chewy scallops. It is also important that you don't overcrowd the scallops in the skillet. If the skillet is not large enough to accommodate scallops in one layer with space between each, sauté them in two batches. Otherwise they will not sauté properly. And remember, fresh basil should always be chopped or julienned just before using, as it will turn brown if done so prematurely. Enjoy!

6 tablespoons butter or olive oil
1 large onion, finely chopped
3 cloves garlic
3 tablespoons all-purpose flour
2 cups heavy cream
1 cup milk
½ cup pesto, homemade (recipe follows) or purchased
Salt and freshly ground black pepper, to taste
¾ cup finely grated Parmigiano-Reggiano cheese

1½ pounds fresh sea scallops, rinsed and patted dry
1 pound dried rotelle
½ cup toasted pine nuts, for garnish
Handful of fresh basil leaves, washed, dried, and julienned, for garnish

In a medium saucepan, melt 2 tablespoons of the butter over medium-high heat. Add the onion and sauté until tender and just beginning to brown around the edges, 5 to 7 minutes. Add garlic and cook another minute, stirring constantly so the garlic doesn't scorch. Add flour, and cook another minute, stirring constantly. Do not allow the flour to brown. Whisk in the heavy cream and bring the sauce to a boil, stirring frequently. Reduce the heat to low and simmer, uncovered, 10 to 15 minutes, or until sauce is quite thick. Whisk in the pesto, season with salt and pepper, and cook about 5 minutes, stirring occasionally. Remove from the heat and, if necessary, thin with a little water. Stir in ¼ cup of the grated cheese.

Melt the remaining 4 tablespoons butter in a large skillet or sauté pan over medium-high heat. Just as the butter begins to brown, add the scallops and quickly sauté, browning on both sides, 2 to 3 minutes per side. Remove from the heat and set aside, lightly covered, to keep warm.

In a kettle or large saucepan, bring 5 quarts of salted water to a boil. Add pasta and return to a boil, stirring occasionally. Cook, stirring occasionally, until the pasta is al dente, 13 to 15 minutes.

Drain the pasta in a colander, then transfer to a large bowl and toss with half of the sauce. Serve with remaining sauce ladled on top, garnished with the sautéed scallops, toasted pine nuts, and julienned fresh basil. Pass the remaining ½ cup grated cheese at the table.

SERVES 4 TO 6

Pesto

2 cloves garlic, pressed or minced
3 cups packed fresh basil leaves
¾ teaspoon salt
½ cup finely grated Parmigiano-Reggiano cheese
2 tablespoons finely grated romano cheese
1 cup extra-virgin olive oil
¼ cup lightly toasted pine nuts
½ cup lightly toasted walnuts
Freshly ground black pepper, to taste

In the bowl of a food processor, combine the garlic, basil leaves, salt, and cheeses. Pulse several times to chop basil, then add the oil in a thin, steady stream while the processor is running. Process until smooth. Add the pine nuts and walnuts and pulse several times, until nuts are incorporated and chopped but pieces are still visible. Taste, adding additional salt if necessary and season with black pepper. The pesto can be frozen in a small, air-tight container for up to 3 months.

MAKES APPROXIMATELY 1¼ CUPS

Spaghetti with Creamy Tomato and Italian Sausage Sauce

I've never really loved spaghetti with meat sauce (except for Mom's), but once I figured out I could make something this good with Italian sausage, I changed my mind. Not at all like a typical meat sauce, this is more like a rich sauce that would be good even without meat, only it has meatball-like pieces of the anise-flavored sweet sausage popping up to surprise you. This is a sauce that people love, is easy to prepare, and can be made well ahead of time.

Sauce

- 2 tablespoons olive oil
- 1 pound sweet Italian sausage, removed from casings and broken into bite-size pieces
- 1 large onion, finely chopped
- 4 cloves garlic, pressed or minced
- 1 medium rib celery, finely chopped
- ½ medium red bell pepper, seeded and coarsely chopped
- ½ medium green bell pepper, seeded and coarsely chopped
- ½ teaspoon crushed red pepper
- 3 tablespoons all-purpose flour
- 1 can (28 ounces) Italian plum tomatoes, undrained and roughly chopped
- 2 cups water
- 2 tablespoons tomato paste
- ½ cup heavy cream
- ¼ cup finely chopped fresh basil or 1 teaspoon dried
- 1 medium or 2 small zucchini, quartered lengthwise and cut crosswise into ½-inch slices
- 4 scallions, thinly sliced
- ⅓ cup fresh or frozen green peas (optional)
- ¼ cup finely minced fresh parsley
- Salt and freshly ground black pepper, to taste
- 1 teaspoon sugar, if needed

1 pound dried spaghetti or linguine
Finely grated Parmigiano-Reggiano cheese, for serving

In a 2½-quart enameled or other nonreactive saucepan, heat the oil over medium-high heat. Add the sausage and brown well. Remove the sausage from the saucepan with a slotted spoon and set aside.

Add the onion, garlic, celery, red and green bell peppers, and crushed red pepper to the saucepan and sauté over medium-high heat until the vegetables are tender and beginning to caramelize around the edges, 5 to 7 minutes, stirring frequently. Sprinkle the flour over the vegetables and cook 1 minute, stirring constantly. Stir in the sausage, tomatoes, water, tomato paste, heavy cream, and basil and bring to a boil. Reduce the heat to low once the sauce begins to thicken and simmer, uncovered, 20 minutes.

Add the zucchini, scallions, peas if desired, and parsley, and cook another 10 minutes. Taste and season with salt and pepper, adding sugar if necessary.

In a kettle or large saucepan, bring 5 quarts of salted water to a boil. Add the pasta and return to a boil, stirring occasionally. Cook, stirring occasionally, until the pasta is al dente, 10 to 12 minutes.

Drain the pasta in a colander, then transfer to a large bowl and toss with half of the sauce. Serve with remaining sauce ladled on top and pass the grated cheese at the table.

SERVES 4 TO 6

Vermicelli with Chicken Liver and Spicy Tomato Sauce

Here is a rich, hearty pasta sauce for those of us lucky enough to be liver lovers. You know who you are. It's a wonderful way to use that part of the chicken which often ends up tossed aside as something unworthy of attention. I like this best with vermicelli or cappellini.

Sauce

¼ cup olive oil
1 large or 2 medium onions, chopped
10 cloves garlic, pressed or minced
1½ pints chicken livers, rinsed, drained, and cut into
    individual lobes
4 pounds fresh, ripe Italian plum tomatoes, coarsely
    chopped, or 2 cans (28 ounces each) crushed Italian
    tomatoes
½ cup finely chopped fresh basil or 1 teaspoon dried,
    crumbled
½ teaspoon crushed red pepper
1 bay leaf
Freshly ground black pepper, to taste
1½ cups chicken stock (or 1½ cups water plus 1 chicken
    bouillon cube)
Salt to taste
1 teaspoon sugar, if needed

1 pound dried vermicelli
½ cup finely grated Parmigiano-Reggiano cheese, for
    serving

In a large, heavy skillet, heat the oil over medium-high heat and sauté onion and garlic until onions are tender and begin to caramelize around the edges, about 5 minutes. Add the chicken livers and cook until they are lightly browned on the outside but not cooked through, about 5 minutes. Remove the livers from skillet, leaving as much of the onion and garlic in the pan as possible, and set aside.

Add the tomatoes, basil, crushed red pepper, bay leaf, black pepper, and chicken stock to the skillet. Stir well, then let the sauce come to a simmer. Cook for 15 to 20 minutes, until most of the liquid has evaporated.

Return the chicken livers and any accumulated drippings to the skillet and stir well. Cook 2 to 3 minutes longer (unless you like your livers very well done), until livers are heated through. Season with salt and pepper, and, if sauce seems overly acidic, add sugar as necessary.

In a kettle or large saucepan, bring 5 quarts of salted water to a boil. Add the pasta and return to a boil, stirring occasionally. Cook, stirring occasionally, until the pasta is al dente, about 4 to 6 minutes.

Drain the pasta in a colander, then transfer to a large bowl. Remove the bay leaf from the sauce before tossing it with the pasta. Spoon the chicken livers over the top of the pasta and serve immediately, passing the grated cheese at the table.

SERVES 4 TO 6

Extraordinary Entrées

The collection of recipes in this section come from quite a variety of sources: some directly from my grandmothers, some from people I've known or places I've been along the way, some which have come into existence because of a particular fondness I have for a certain ingredient. The unifying factor is that they are all dishes I consider not-to-be-missed items in my repertoire. They range from formal and impressive to simple home-cooking at its best. I have loosely grouped the recipes by basic food types: vegetables, seafood, chicken, and meat. And, whenever appropriate I have noted the dishes that could serve as appetizers.

Laissez les bons temps rouler.

Vegetables

Stuffed Artichokes with Tomato Gravy
Red Beans and Rice with Green Tomato and Onion Relish
Creole Eggplant or Mirliton
Wild Mushroom Risotto
Okra Gumbo
Torta di Palmito

Stuffed Artichokes with Tomato Gravy

I must say that this is a very unusual way to prepare artichokes, though it wasn't until much after I left home that I realized this. Stuffed artichokes are quite common, but I have never seen them stuffed with a meat mixture as in this recipe, which comes from MaMa LaChute. She didn't make them very often, as they do demand a certain amount of time to prepare, but when she did find the time, she would make enough for everyone. The news would spread through the family quickly, and all of my aunts and uncles would flock back home to pick up their allotments.

These are absolutely delicious. Be forewarned, however: They are difficult to eat in a formal setting—a lot of dripping and finger-licking is required. I have had people suggest that bibs may be in order . . . Oh, well. As far as I'm concerned, that's part of the fun. MaMa usually serves the artichokes on top of pasta, with sweet tomato gravy ladled over all.

Stuffing

2 pounds ground beef chuck
1¼ cups unseasoned dry bread crumbs
12 cloves garlic, pressed or minced
½ bunch scallions, chopped
1½ medium onions, finely chopped
4 large eggs
⅓ cup chopped fresh parsley
1½ teaspoons salt
½ teaspoon cayenne pepper

Tomato Gravy

¼ cup olive or canola oil
1½ medium onions, finely chopped
10 cloves garlic, pressed or minced
½ medium green bell pepper, seeded and finely chopped
½ bunch scallions, chopped
3 cans (6 ounces each) tomato paste
1 can (35 ounces) puréed Italian tomatoes

1 tablespoon dried basil, crumbled
1 teaspoon dried oregano, crumbled
½ cup sugar
8 cups water
Salt and freshly ground black pepper, to taste

6 large artichokes, stems trimmed flush with bottoms
1 lemon, halved
1 pound spaghetti, cooked

Combine all the stuffing ingredients in a large bowl and mix with your hands until thoroughly blended. Keep refrigerated while you prepare the tomato gravy.

Select a very large saucepan or roasting pan (the pan should be large enough to hold gravy and all the artichokes in one layer once stuffed. If you don't have one pan large enough, make the sauce in a large saucepan and then divide it between two pans in which the artichokes will fit). In it, heat the oil over medium heat. Add the onions, garlic, bell pepper, and scallions and sauté until tender, about 5 minutes. Add the tomato paste, tomato purée, basil, oregano, sugar, 8 cups water, and salt and pepper and bring to a boil. Reduce the heat to medium-low and simmer, uncovered, until the flavors have come together and the sauce has reduced by one fourth, about 30 minutes.

While the sauce is simmering, prepare the artichokes. Remove all blemished outer leaves of the artichokes and trim the stems so they are flush with the bottoms of the artichokes and the artichokes stand upright. Trim off the upper fourth of each artichoke, then snip off the tips of all the leaves to remove the thorns. Rub the artichokes all over with a lemon half. This will prevent the artichokes from discoloring. With your hands, gently loosen the artichoke leaves by pulling them apart—this will make stuffing much easier.

Beginning with the outermost leaves, stuff the meat mixture between as many leaves as possible, using about a tablespoon of meat mixture per leaf. At a certain point toward the center of the artichoke, you will no longer be able to pry the leaves apart. At this point, go on to the next one.

Once you have all the artichokes stuffed, place them directly in the pot with the hot tomato gravy and cook slowly either on top of the stove or in a 350°F oven (I find they are less likely to scorch on the bottom if you are able to cook them in the oven) until they are quite tender, an hour and a half or so (see Note).

Serve the artichokes and sauce over the cooked spaghetti.

SERVES 6 GENEROUSLY

NOTE: The artichokes should be completely covered with the gravy. If they are not, add enough water to the gravy so that it covers them. Once the artichokes are cooked, you will need to remove them from the gravy while you reduce it to a proper serving consistency.

Red Beans and Rice with Green Tomato and Onion Relish

Red beans and rice is a dish so integral to my food life that it is inconceivable to me to not include it in my first collection of recipes. I like to make it on a Monday, the day it is usually prepared in New Orleans. This tradition supposedly derives from the fact that Monday was always laundry day in the Crescent City, and red beans could be put on to cook in the morning and left to simmer away all day long with next to no attention, leaving the cook free to her laundry duties. It is also traditional to have a bottle of hot sauce on the table, either Tabasco or Louisiana Red Hot, as well as a bottle of peppered vinegar and a loaf of hot crusty French bread with butter. I have developed a personal tradition of enjoying them with a relish made of green tomatoes and onion, so I have included the recipe for that here as well.

1 pound dried red kidney beans
1 pound smoked sausage, such as kielbasa, sliced into
    ½-inch rounds
1 smoked ham hock, skin slit in several places
1 medium rib celery, chopped
2 medium onions, chopped
6 cloves garlic, pressed or minced
1 bay leaf
1 teaspoon ground allspice
1 teaspoon crushed red pepper
6 cups water, plus more as needed
¼ cup chopped fresh parsley
½ bunch scallions, chopped
Salt and cayenne pepper, to taste
Cooked white rice, for serving
Green Tomato and Onion Relish (recipe follows), for
    serving

Rinse and pick over the beans. Place in a large saucepan with enough water to cover by 2 inches. Bring to a boil over high heat, then reduce the heat to low and simmer for 10 minutes. Cover the pot and remove it from the heat. Let the beans sit for at least 1 hour.

While the beans are sitting, sauté the sausage slices in a large, heavy skillet over medium-high heat until browned on all sides, 1 to 2 minutes per side. Using a slotted spoon, remove from the skillet and set aside.

Add the ham hock, celery, and onions to the skillet and continue to cook over medium-high heat until the vegetables are tender and the slits in the hock begin to open, 7 to 8 minutes. Add the garlic and cook 1 minute, stirring constantly so the garlic won't scorch. Add the bay leaf, allspice, and crushed red pepper, stirring well to mix.

Drain the beans, then return them to their pot. Add the sautéed sausage, vegetables, ham hock, and 6 cups water and bring to a boil over high heat. Skim off any froth or scum that rises to the surface. Cover the pot, reduce the heat to low, and simmer 2 to 3 hours, uncovering occasionally to stir. The amount of time needed will vary depending on the beans. After 1½ hours, check to make sure the beans have not dried out, and add water as needed.

When the beans are cooked to the desired consistency, season with salt and pepper. Salting the cooking water any earlier than this will toughen the skin of the beans. Add the parsley and scallions and simmer 10 minutes longer. Remove the bay leaf before serving.

Serve over rice, accompanied by Green Tomato and Onion Relish (see Note).

SERVES 4 TO 6

NOTE: Red beans are always better the next day or after being frozen. If you prepare them ahead of time, take care to reheat them over low heat, stirring frequently to prevent scorching. Also, beans prepared ahead of time will almost always need to be thinned with a little water.

Green Tomato and Onion Relish

5 pounds green tomatoes, cored and sliced
4 large onions, peeled and sliced
Kosher salt
3 red bell peppers, seeded and finely chopped
1 pound light brown sugar, or to taste
1 cup granulated sugar
2 cups distilled white vinegar
2 cups cider vinegar
1½ tablespoons ground cinnamon
1 tablespoon ground allspice
½ teaspoon ground cloves
1 teaspoon crushed red pepper (optional)

In a large glass bowl or casserole dish, layer the sliced tomatoes and onions and sprinkle each layer generously with kosher salt. Cover and refrigerate overnight.

Drain the tomatoes and onions and place in a large enameled or other nonreactive saucepan. Add the remaining ingredients and bring to a boil. Reduce the heat to low and let simmer until the vegetables are tender, usually 30 minutes.

Remove from the heat and spoon the relish into hot, sterilized jars. Process jars in a hot water bath to seal. Cool and store in a cool, dark place up to 1 year.

MAKES ABOUT 3 QUARTS

Creole Eggplant or Mirliton

This is a traditional Creole dish which can be prepared with either eggplant or mirliton, whichever you happen to be able to get your hands on. Mirlitons (pronounced *mehl-i-tawn*), which are also known as chayote or christophene, are my favorite vegetable to prepare in this way, but they are sometimes difficult to find in the grocery. As they are a vegetable used a lot in Mexican and South and Central American cooking, you can usually find them in specialty supermarkets. Actually a type of squash, they resemble flattened pears, and have a light green skin, which is often prickly. I think they are well worth the extra effort you may have to go to in order to find them.

3 tablespoons butter
3 large eggplants or 5 mirlitons
2 medium onions, finely chopped
4 cloves garlic, pressed or finely chopped
½ bunch scallions, chopped
1½ pounds medium shrimp, peeled, deveined, and finely
  chopped
1¼ cups unseasoned dry bread crumbs
2 large eggs
½ cup chopped fresh parsley
Salt and cayenne pepper, to taste
8 ounces Cheddar or American cheese, grated
6 cups cooked white rice, for serving
Tabasco or other hot pepper sauce, for serving

If you are using eggplants, peel them and cut into 2-inch chunks. Boil the eggplant pieces in salted water until very soft, usually about 15 minutes. If you are using mirlitons, see the Note below.

In a skillet, melt the butter over medium heat. Add the onions, garlic, and scallions and sauté until tender, about 5 minutes. Remove from the heat and set aside.

Preheat the oven to 350°F.

In a colander, drain the eggplant well, then mash in a bowl or purée in a food processor. Add the eggplant to the sautéed vegetables in the skillet and cook for 10 minutes or so to reduce the amount of liquid, stirring constantly. Add the shrimp and cook until they begin to turn pink. Remove from the heat and stir in 1 cup of the bread crumbs, the eggs, parsley, and salt and pepper.

Spoon the seasoned eggplant mixture into a casserole dish and top with the grated cheese. Sprinkle with the remaining ¼ cup bread crumbs and bake for 30 to 45 minutes, until hot throughout and the cheese is melted and bread crumbs lightly browned.

Serve with cooked rice, and make sure to have some hot sauce on the table.

SERVES 6

NOTE: You can prepare mirlitons the same way. Because they are so much smaller than the eggplants I use here, you can reserve the mirliton shells and use these in place of a casserole dish. This makes a nice presentation, with one or two individual stuffed mirliton halves making one serving. Follow the directions above, but boil the mirlitons whole until soft (check by piercing with a knife). Cut them in half after cooking and scoop out the flesh (I find a melon-baller works well for this) after removing the almond-shaped seed in the middle. Leave a ¼-inch border of flesh to support the thin shell. Proceed from here as directed.

Wild Mushroom Risotto

I must confess a particular fondness for risotto. The porcini mushrooms serve to create a rich stock which just screams mushrooms, and the result is hearty risotto which can serve as a complete meal in itself, although it is also a great accompaniment to roast chicken or meat.

½ ounce dried porcini mushrooms
6½ cups water
1 chicken bouillon cube
6 tablespoons butter
½ cup olive oil
8 ounces fresh shiitake mushrooms, sliced
8 ounces fresh button or cremini mushrooms, sliced
Salt and freshly ground black pepper, to taste
3 large portobello mushrooms, trimmed and cut into
   ⅓-inch slices
1 medium onion, finely chopped
½ medium red bell pepper, seeded and finely chopped
2 shallots, minced
1⅔ cups Arborio rice
½ cup dry red or white wine
1 teaspoon dried thyme, crumbled
½ cup fresh or frozen green peas
1 bunch scallions, green tops only, thinly sliced
Hot water, if needed
1½ cups grated Parmigiano-Reggiano cheese
⅓ cup heavy cream

In a medium saucepan, combine the dried porcini mushrooms with the water and chicken bouillon cube and bring to a boil for 2 minutes, then remove from the heat and let stand.

In a large skillet, melt 4 tablespoons of the butter over medium heat. Add the shiitake and button or cremini mushrooms and sauté until soft and golden brown around the edges, 5 to 6 minutes. Remove from the heat and season with salt and pepper, then transfer mushrooms to a bowl and set aside. In the same skillet, heat ¼ cup of the olive oil, still over medium heat, and sauté the portobello mushrooms until softened and golden brown around the edges, 5 to 6 minutes. Season with salt and pepper, remove from the heat, and set aside.

Strain the porcini stock through a fine sieve and return the stock to a simmer. Finely chop the mushrooms and set aside.

In a large, heavy saucepan, heat the remaining ¼ cup olive oil and 2 tablespoons butter over medium-high heat. Add the onion, bell pepper, and shallots and sauté until tender, 3 to 5 minutes. Add the rice (do not rinse) and cook 2 to 3 minutes, stirring constantly, until it becomes opaque. Add the wine and stir until the rice has completely absorbed all the liquid.

Stir the thyme, reserved porcini mushrooms, and sautéed shiitake and button mushrooms into the rice, then begin adding porcini stock in ½-cup increments, stirring constantly and letting the rice completely absorb the liquid between additions until the rice is tender, usually about 20 minutes. Add the peas and scallion tops 15 minutes after you begin cooking the rice. If you use all the stock before the rice is completely cooked, add a bit of hot water. The rice should be slightly al dente, although this is a matter of personal taste.

When the rice is done, add 1 cup of the grated cheese and the heavy cream and stir well to mix. Taste and season with salt and pepper. Serve immediately, garnished with the warm sautéed portobellos and the remaining grated cheese.

SERVES 4 AS AN ENTRÉE, 6 TO 8 AS AN APPETIZER

Okra Gumbo

Not for the okra-shy among us, this is a very traditional rendering of a Creole classic. For a gumbo, it is exceedingly simple to make and healthful, too, as it needs no roux to serve as thickener—the okra takes care of that all by itself.

¼ cup canola oil
1 large onion, finely chopped
2 packages (10 ounces each) frozen chopped okra
1½ teaspoons distilled white vinegar
3 ounces tomato paste
1½ pounds small or medium shrimp, peeled and deveined
5 cups water
Salt and cayenne pepper, to taste
Tabasco to taste (optional)

6 cups cooked white rice, as an accompaniment

In a large cast-iron skillet or heavy saucepan, heat canola oil over medium-high heat. Add onion, okra and vinegar and cook, stirring frequently, until okra is an olive green color, about 25 minutes. Add tomato paste, stirring well to mix, and cook another 2 minutes. Add shrimp and cook until they turn pink, 4 to 5 minutes. Add water and bring to a simmer. Reduce heat to low and simmer until gumbo is thick and shrimp are tender, 45 minutes to 1 hour. Taste and season with salt and cayenne. Add Tabasco if desired and serve in bowls over hot, cooked white rice.

SERVES 4

Torta di Palmito

In English, this is "heart of palm torte." If you are fond of this delicacy, you will ooh and ah over this torte. The recipe comes to me from my Brazilian friend Judith. She says she's never served it to anyone who has not liked it. The tender, flaky crust is loaded with Parmesan cheese, and the filling is made rich and creamy by a béchamel. This is easily a meal in itself when served alongside a simple green salad, although Judith says it is traditionally eaten with rice in Brazil.

Pastry

1¼ cups unbleached all-purpose flour
½ teaspoon salt
1 cup finely grated Parmigiano-Reggiano cheese
8 tablespoons cold butter, cut into small pieces
3 tablespoons ice-cold water, or more as needed

Filling

8 tablespoons butter
½ medium onion, finely chopped
½ medium green bell pepper, seeded and finely chopped
1 medium rib celery, finely chopped
2 cloves garlic, pressed or minced
3 fresh, ripe medium tomatoes, cored and chopped
1 tablespoon fresh basil or parsley, finely chopped
6 tablespoons unbleached all-purpose flour
1 can (12 ounces) evaporated milk
2 jars (15 ounces each) hearts of palm, drained and cut
   crosswise into ½-inch slices
1 cup Spanish or Kalamata olives, coarsely chopped
Salt and freshly ground black pepper, to taste

Make the pastry: In a medium bowl, combine the flour, salt, and grated cheese. Add the butter pieces, and using a pastry blender, two knives, or your fingertips, cut the butter into the dry ingredients until the mixture resembles coarse crumbs. Sprinkle the mixture with the ice water and toss with a fork to mix. Knead briefly, only until the pastry comes together. If it seems dry, add a bit more water. Shape into a flattened disc shape and refrigerate, wrapped in plastic, for at least 1 hour while you prepare the filling.

In a medium saucepan, melt the butter over medium heat. Add the onion, bell pepper, celery, and garlic and cook until tender, about 5 minutes. Add the tomatoes and cook, uncovered, until thickened and most of the liquid has evaporated, about 15 minutes. Add the basil and season with salt and pepper. Remove from the heat and set aside.

In a second medium saucepan, melt the butter over medium heat and whisk in the flour. Cook 1 minute but do not allow the flour to brown. Slowly whisk in the evaporated milk until thoroughly blended. Continue to cook over medium heat, whisking constantly, until the mixture is quite thick, about 5 minutes. Remove from the heat and set the béchamel aside.

Remove the pastry from the refrigerator.

Butter a 2-quart casserole or soufflé dish and set aside. In a large bowl, combine the sliced hearts of palm, olives, and reserved tomato and béchamel sauces, and using a spatula, gently fold the ingredients together. Season with salt and pepper, transfer the mixture to the prepared casserole dish and set aside.

Preheat the oven to 350°F.

On a lightly floured surface, roll the pastry out to a thickness of ¼ inch in the shape of the casserole dish you are using. Carefully transfer the pastry to the top of the casserole dish and trim pastry so that it is slightly larger than the casserole dish. Ease edges into casserole on top of filling and decorate or crimp the pastry as desired.

Bake the torte in the middle of the oven for 20 to 25 minutes, or until the pastry is golden brown and the filling is heated through.

SERVES 6

Seafood

Catfish Po-Boys
Crab Cakes with Two Sauces
Crawfish Pie
Baked Halibut in Fennel-Saffron Broth
Shrimp Creole
New Orleans–Style Barbecued Shrimp
Shrimp Risotto

Catfish Po-Boys

I know many folks who are prejudiced against catfish: They claim that since catfish are "bottom dwellers" that they taste "dirty." But good, fresh catfish are a treat in the South, and because they have become so well loved across the country, most of the catfish we find in seafood markets today are farm-raised anyway. Perhaps they should be reconsidered.

There is one surefire way to make a believer out of you, but that would involve a trip to Pass Manchac, Louisiana, to Middendorf's, a restaurant that has been there for many, many moons. Folks come from all over to have their fried catfish, which comes two different ways: thick or thin. When my PaPa Armstrong was feeling frisky he'd host a pilgrimage to Middendorf's, and being the gentleman he was, he'd make sure I had as many Shirley Temples as I cared to have, while he sat and satisfied his hunger for catfish. There is no way I could begin to claim to make catfish like they do at Middendorf's. However, I think that if you're nowhere near the vicinity of Pass Manchac and you find yourself with a craving for catfish, try my recipe here for a good old-fashioned catfish po-boy. Miss Myrtle's Coleslaw (page 178) would be the perfect accompaniment.

Catfish

½ cup Louisiana Red Hot
3 tablespoons Dijon mustard
2 pounds catfish fillets, cut into thin strips for frying
2 cups cornmeal
½ cup all-purpose flour
2 teaspoons Tony Chachere's Creole Seasoning
1 teaspoon salt
1 teaspoon garlic powder
2 teaspoons cayenne pepper
6 to 8 cups vegetable oil for deep frying

Po-Boys

2 loaves French bread, sliced lengthwise and cut into
   desired lengths
Lemon wedges
Louisiana Red Hot or Tabasco
½ cup butter, melted to brush on bread
Lettuce (optional)
Sliced tomato (optional)
Homemade Tartar Sauce (page 91 optional)

Combine the Louisiana Red Hot and mustard in a glass or
stainless-steel bowl or plastic bag and add the catfish, tossing the
strips to coat. Marinate the catfish for at least 1 hour, refrigerated.

While the catfish is marinating, combine the cornmeal,
flour, and seasonings in a large plastic bag.

In a heavy kettle or skillet, heat the oil to 375°F (test with a
deep-fry thermometer).

Remove the catfish strips from the marinade. Wipe off any
excess liquid with your hands, dredge in the seasoned cornmeal
mixture, and fry in the hot oil until the strips are golden brown all
over and they float to the top of the oil. Do this in batches, making
sure not to overcrowd the kettle. The cooking time will vary, depending on the size and thickness of the strips you are using.

Remove the catfish to paper towels to drain while you dress
the bread. It is most traditional to eat catfish po-boys on warm,
buttered French bread with hot sauce. However, lettuce and
tomato are fine accompaniments, as is tartar sauce.

SERVES 4 TO 6

Crab Cakes with Two Sauces

These crab cakes are the real thing, with very little in the way of filler other than seasonings and a small amount of bread crumbs. For this reason they can be a bit fragile to handle, but if you take your time when sautéing them, you will be knocked over by the results—a thin, crispy coating around creamy, well-seasoned crabmeat. I like to serve them with both the sauces that follow.

It is important that you take the time needed to pick over the crabmeat very well—there is nothing as frustrating as having a mouthful of delicious crab cake and having to interrupt the process to search out an errant crab shell.

5 tablespoons butter
1 large onion, finely chopped
½ medium red bell pepper, seeded and finely chopped
½ bunch scallions, finely chopped
1 medium rib celery, finely chopped
2 cloves garlic, pressed or minced
¼ teaspoon crushed red pepper
½ teaspoon dried thyme, crumbled
1 pound lump crabmeat, picked over for shells
1 large egg, lightly beaten
2 tablespoons heavy cream
2 tablespoons mayonnaise
¼ cup chopped fresh parsley
1 cup unseasoned dry bread crumbs
¼ teaspoon Tony Chachere's Creole Seasoning
¼ teaspoon salt
Freshly ground black pepper, to taste
¼ cup canola oil
Roasted Red Pepper Sauce (recipe follows)
Homemade Tartar Sauce (recipe follows)

In a large skillet, heat 3 tablespoons of the butter over medium heat. Add the onion, bell pepper, scallions, and celery and sauté until tender. Add the garlic, crushed red pepper, and thyme and cook 1 to 2 minutes longer. Remove from the heat. Transfer the mixture to a bowl and cool to room temperature, 20 to 30 minutes.

When the seasoning mixture is completely cool, add the crabmeat, egg, heavy cream, mayonnaise, Creole seasoning, salt, parsley, ¼ cup of the bread crumbs, and pepper. Mix quickly but thoroughly, then form into ¾-inch cakes about 2½ inches wide (a ¼- or ⅓-cup measuring cup or ice cream scoop will work fine for this). Spread the remaining bread crumbs on a plate and dredge the cakes in them to coat completely.

Heat the skillet over medium-high heat and add canola oil. When it is hot, add the remaining 2 tablespoons butter and sauté the crab cakes until golden brown and crispy on both sides, 2 to 3 minutes per side. Serve with Roasted Red Pepper Sauce and Homemade Tartar Sauce.

SERVES 4

Roasted Red Pepper Sauce

4 red bell peppers
2 tablespoons olive oil or butter
1 medium onion, finely chopped
4 cloves garlic, pressed or minced
¼ teaspoon dried thyme, crumbled
½ teaspoon crushed red pepper
½ cup chicken stock, homemade or canned broth
¼ cup heavy cream, or as needed
Salt, to taste
Few drops of fresh lemon juice
1 teaspoon sugar (optional)

If you have gas burners, roast the peppers by placing them directly on top of the burners, with the gas on high, turning them with tongs so they become completely black and charred all over (see Note). Place them in a plastic or paper bag and close tightly. Let them steam for 15 to 20 minutes to loosen the skins.

When the peppers are cool enough to handle, rub the charred outer skin off the peppers. Try to do this without running them under water, as this will wash away a lot of the charred flavor. Remove the stems, inner cores, and seeds from the peppers, then tear them into strips and set aside.

In a medium saucepan, heat the oil over medium heat. Add the onion and sauté until tender, about 5 minutes. Add the roasted peppers, garlic, thyme, and crushed red pepper and cook 1 to 2 minutes. Add the chicken stock and bring to a simmer. Cook, uncovered, for 10 to 15 minutes, until the peppers are very tender and most of the liquid has evaporated. Transfer the contents of the pan to a blender, and adding only as much cream as is necessary, purée the sauce until quite smooth. Return to the saucepan and season with salt and a few drops of lemon juice. Keep warm until serving time.

MAKES ABOUT 2 CUPS

NOTE: If you don't have gas burners, rub peppers all over with cooking oil and broil 5 inches away from heat source, turning frequently, until skin is charred and blistered all over. Remove from oven and place in plastic or paper bag or airtight container and proceed as directed above.

Homemade Tartar Sauce

1 cup mayonnaise, preferably homemade
1 teaspoon Dijon mustard
2 scallions, finely chopped
1 clove garlic, pressed or minced
1 shallot, finely chopped
1 tablespoon capers, drained and finely chopped
2 tablespoons chopped cornichons or dill pickle
⅛ teaspoon cayenne pepper
1 tablespoon chopped fresh parsley
Salt, to taste
Pinch of dried tarragon (optional), crumbled

Combine all the ingredients in a bowl. Refrigerate until serving time. Serve with hot crab cakes.

MAKES ABOUT 1½ CUPS

Crawfish Pie

One of the best ways to eat "mudbugs" that I know of. If you don't happen to be lucky enough to live in a place where crawfish are readily available, try asking your local seafood market whether they can get them for you. Usually this is not a problem if crawfish are in season; they are available in 1-pound bags, vacuum packed and already peeled for you, ready to use in any way you desire.

6 tablespoons butter
6 tablespoons all-purpose flour
1 large onion, finely chopped
1 medium rib celery, finely chopped
½ green bell pepper, seeded and finely chopped
4 cloves garlic, pressed or minced
2 bunches scallions, tops separated from bottoms,
    both chopped
1½ tablespoons tomato paste
½ teaspoon dried thyme, crumbled
½ teaspoon dried basil, crumbled
1 teaspoon Worcestershire sauce
1 teaspoon salt
½ teaspoon cayenne or crushed red pepper
½ teaspoon freshly ground black pepper
3 cups water
1½ fish bouillon cubes
Basic Pie Crust, made as described for savory dishes
    (page 233)
3 pounds cleaned crawfish tails, with the fat
1 teaspoon fresh lemon juice
½ cup chopped parsley

Make a roux by melting the butter in a large, heavy skillet or saucepan over medium heat, then whisking in the flour. Cook over medium heat, stirring constantly, until the roux is a medium brown color, about 5 to 10 minutes.

Add the onion, celery, bell pepper, and garlic to the hot roux and stir well to mix. Reduce the heat and cook until the vegetables are wilted, about 5 minutes. Add the chopped bottom portion of scallions and cook another 3 minutes, then add the tomato paste and cook 2 to 3 minutes more, stirring constantly. Stir in the thyme, basil, Worcestershire sauce, salt, cayenne pepper, black pepper, water, and bouillon cubes and simmer, uncovered, until the flavors come together, about 1 hour, until reduced by a third.

Prepare the pie crust and let it chill in the refrigerator while the crawfish filling simmers.

After the vegetable and roux mixture has simmered 1 hour, add crawfish tails and fat, lemon juice, parsley, and chopped scallion tops and simmer 10 more minutes.

Meanwhile, preheat the oven to 375°F.

Taste the filling, adjusting the seasoning if necessary, and remove from the heat. Pour the filling into a 2-quart soufflé dish. Roll out the pastry to fit the top of the dish, tucking in the edges and cutting several vents in the top for steam to escape. Bake for 45 minutes, or until the filling is hot and bubbly and the pastry is golden brown.

SERVES 6

Baked Halibut in Fennel-Saffron Broth

Halibut is something I had to leave New Orleans to discover, but it is a fish I have come to like quite a lot. Extremely light and fresh-tasting, halibut is also very easy to prepare and is often liked even by non–fish lovers. What follows is a sort of variation on the bouillabaisse concept, in which fillets of halibut are baked in the oven in a matter of minutes, only to emerge tender, moist and flaky, then to be combined with braised fennel and topped with a soothing broth. I think the best accompaniment to this dish is garlic mashed potatoes. Mound the potatoes in the center of a low-sided bowl, with the halibut and fennel resting on top and the broth ladled over all.

Broth

3 tablespoons olive oil
1 large onion, thinly sliced
2 medium ribs celery, cut thinly on the diagonal
8 cloves garlic, smashed with the side of a knife and peeled
¼ cup tomato paste
3 pinches saffron threads
8 cups fish or shrimp stock (or 8 cups water and 2 fish bouillon cubes)
2 chicken bouillon cubes
¼ teaspoon crushed red pepper
Juice of half an orange
1 strip (3 inches) orange peel
2 fennel bulbs, cut crosswise into ½-inch slices
Salt and freshly ground black pepper, to taste

6 portions (6 ounces each) halibut fillet
2 tablespoons butter
Salt and freshly ground black pepper, to taste

In a large saucepan, heat the oil over low heat. Add the onion, celery, and garlic and cook until tender, 6 to 8 minutes. Stir in the tomato paste, saffron, stock, bouillon cubes, crushed red pepper, orange juice, and orange peel and bring to a simmer. Cook, uncovered, for 1 hour, until the liquid is reduced by a third.

Add the fennel and continue to simmer until the fennel is tender, about 20 minutes. Add the salt and pepper to taste. Keep warm while preparing the halibut.

Preheat the oven to 425°F.

Place the halibut pieces in one layer in a shallow baking dish or on a baking sheet with low sides. Add enough broth just to cover the bottom of the baking dish. Place a slice of butter on top of every piece of halibut, season with salt and pepper, and loosely cover with a sheet of kitchen parchment paper or foil. Bake for 5 minutes, then remove the parchment and continue to cook another 5 minutes or so, until the fish is cooked through and flakes easily. Be careful not to overcook the fish.

Working carefully and using a wide metal spatula, remove the pieces of halibut to shallow soup plates. Serve immediately, with broth and fennel ladled over fish.

SERVES 6

Shrimp Creole

This is a great dish to make for dinner parties. You can make the sauce in advance and simply reheat it when it's time for dinner, adding the shrimp at the last minute. It is best served with a loaf of hot, crusty French bread or homemade biscuits and a simple green salad. Be careful not to over-cook the shrimp—they will become tough and chewy if you do.

Shrimp Stock

2 pounds medium shrimp
2½ cups water
1 medium rib celery cut into 2-inch lengths
1 medium onion, quartered

6 tablespoons butter
6 tablespoons all-purpose flour
2 medium onions, chopped
1 medium rib celery, chopped
½ medium green bell pepper, chopped
6 cloves garlic, pressed or minced
1 teaspoon crushed red pepper, or to taste
1 can (6 ounces) tomato paste
1 tablespoon sugar
1 can (35 ounces) Italian plum tomatoes, undrained and
    broken up with your hands
1 teaspoon dried oregano, crumbled
¾ teaspoon dried basil, crumbled
¾ teaspoon dried thyme, crumbled
1 bay leaf
Salt and freshly ground black pepper, to taste
1 teaspoon grated lemon zest
1 teaspoon Worcestershire sauce
3 dashes Tabasco or other hot pepper sauce, plus additional
    for serving
1 bunch scallions, finely chopped

¼ cup chopped fresh parsley
6 to 8 cups hot, cooked white rice, for serving

Make the stock. Shell and devein the shrimp. Set the shrimp aside and refrigerate for later use. Combine the shells, water, celery, and quartered onion in a medium saucepan. Simmer mixture 15 to 20 minutes. Remove from the heat and strain the stock through a fine-meshed sieve. Set aside. Discard the shells and vegetables in the sieve.

In a large enameled or other nonreactive saucepan, melt the butter, then whisk in the flour. Cook over medium heat, stirring constantly, until the roux is a medium brown color, about 5 to 10 minutes. Immediately add the chopped onions, celery, bell pepper, garlic, and crushed red pepper to the roux and cook, still over medium heat, until the vegetables are tender, about 5 minutes. Add the tomato paste and cook another 5 to 10 minutes.

Whisk in the reserved shrimp stock, then add the sugar, tomatoes, oregano, basil, thyme, bay leaf, salt, pepper, lemon zest, Worcestershire, and Tabasco. Bring to a boil, then reduce the heat to low and simmer, uncovered, for 45 minutes to 1 hour, stirring frequently.

Once the flavors have come together and you are satisfied with the thickness of the sauce, add the chopped scallions, parsley, and reserved shrimp and stir well. Continue to simmer only until the shrimp are just done, about 10 minutes. Taste and adjust the seasoning and remove the bay leaf. Serve over hot, cooked white rice, with Tabasco sauce on the side.

SERVES 6

New Orleans–Style Barbecued Shrimp

I am at a loss to tell you just why barbecued shrimp are so named—they are neither grilled nor do they have even a drop of barbecue sauce on them. What I do know, however, is that shrimp are delicious prepared this way, and a lot of folks must agree with me, judging from the fact that almost every traditional New Orleans restaurant has a variation of this dish on its menu. It is of the utmost importance that you have lots of French bread on hand when you serve this, as the delicious butter sauce demands to be dipped and wiped up. Also, this is an eat-at-home-with-familiar-folks dish—the peeling, dipping, and general messiness don't lend themselves well to formal dinner parties.

1 cup (2 sticks) butter
1 large onion, finely chopped
1 bunch scallions, finely chopped
2 medium ribs celery, finely chopped
1 medium green bell pepper, seeded and finely chopped
10 cloves garlic, pressed or minced
½ cup extra-virgin olive oil
½ teaspoon cayenne pepper, or to taste
½ teaspoon freshly ground black pepper
2 tablespoons Worcestershire sauce
Juice of 2 lemons
2 bay leaves
2 teaspoons fresh rosemary, finely chopped
5 pounds medium shrimp, in the shell
Fresh, hot French bread, for serving

Preheat the oven to 300°F.

In a large, heavy skillet, melt the butter over medium-high heat. Add the onion, scallions, celery, bell pepper, and garlic and sauté until tender, about 5 minutes. Add the olive oil, cayenne and black peppers, Worcestershire, lemon juice, bay leaves, and rosemary. Reduce the heat to low, and simmer for 10 minutes.

Pour the butter mixture into a large roasting pan or baking pan. Add the shrimp and mix well. Bake for 25 to 30 minutes, stirring occasionally, until the shrimp are just done. The amount of time it takes until the shrimp are done will vary, depending on the size of shrimp you are using, as well as your oven. The shrimp are done when they have turned pink and the shell begins to pull away from the flesh slightly. Remove the bay leaves and serve the shrimp immediately, with lots of fresh, hot French bread to dip in the juices.

SERVES 6 TO 8

NOTE: The shrimp and sauce are also delicious served over hot linguine or fettuccine.

Shrimp Risotto

If you like rice, you'll love risotto. Don't be intimidated by the cooking process. I find a heavy, enameled Dutch oven works best, but if you have a heavy pot that also has a nonstick finish, it can work just as well. Medium-high heat is a good place to start, but be aware that every stovetop is different. Making risotto is a simple process, provided you are willing to stand and stir for the duration of the cooking time. For this reason, I never serve risotto at a dinner party. This is a dish to make for folks who will enjoy standing in the kitchen with you as you stir, stir, stir. If they are already familiar with the process and the wonderful outcome of a well-tended risotto, they will be happy to help you get everything else ready and on the table while you do your part.

1½ pounds medium shrimp, in the shell
2 teaspoons fresh thyme leaves
4 cloves garlic, pressed or minced
½ teaspoon Tony Chachere's Creole Seasoning
⅔ cup olive oil
2 large onions
1 rib celery, cut into 1-inch slices
6 cups water
6 tablespoons butter
Juice of 1 lemon
1 red bell pepper, seeded and chopped
1½ cups Arborio rice
½ cup dry white wine
2 medium carrots, peeled and finely chopped or grated
3 scallions, chopped
½ cup frozen green peas
½ cup heavy cream
¾ cup freshly grated Parmigiano-Reggiano cheese
Salt and freshly ground black pepper, to taste

Peel and devein the shrimp, reserving the shells. In a small bowl, combine the shrimp, 1 teaspoon of the thyme leaves, half the garlic, the Creole seasoning, and ⅓ cup of the oil. Toss well to coat, then marinate, covered, in the refrigerator for at least 1 hour.

Meanwhile, chop 1½ onions and set aside, cut the remaining onion half in half and combine in a medium saucepan with the celery, reserved shrimp shells, and water. Bring to a boil over high heat, then reduce the heat to low and simmer for 15 minutes. Remove from the heat and strain the stock through a fine-meshed sieve. Return it to the rinsed-out pan and set aside.

Remove the shrimp from the refrigerator. Set a large skillet over medium heat. Add the shrimp and marinade and sauté just until the shrimp turn pink, about 5 minutes. Remove from the heat and stir in 3 tablespoons of the butter and the lemon juice. Set aside.

Return the shrimp stock to a simmer and have a ladle within reach. In a large, heavy saucepan, heat the remaining ⅓ cup oil over medium-high heat. Add the reserved chopped onion, the bell pepper, and remaining garlic and sauté until vegetables are tender, 3 to 5 minutes. Add the rice (do not rinse) and cook 2 to 3 minutes, stirring constantly, until it becomes opaque. Add the wine and stir until the rice has completely absorbed all the liquid. Stir in the remaining teaspoon thyme leaves. From this point on, add the hot stock in ½-cup increments, stirring constantly and adding more stock only as the liquid is absorbed by the rice. After about 10 minutes, add carrots. After 15 minutes, add the chopped scallions and frozen peas.

When the rice starts absorbing less liquid and the raw taste is gone (20 to 25 minutes—the rice should be slightly al dente), stir in the heavy cream, grated cheese, and remaining 3 tablespoons butter. Remove from the heat and season with salt and pepper. Quickly reheat the shrimp and lemon-butter sauce, seasoning with salt and pepper. Serve the risotto immediately, topped with the shrimp and lemon-butter sauce.

SERVES 4 TO 6

Chicken

Southern Fried Chicken with Cream Gravy
Chicken and Dumplings
Chicken and Sausage Gumbo
Pan-Fried Breast of Chicken with Red-Eye Gravy
Chicken Braised with Garlic and Green Olives
Chicken Pot Pie
Roast Chicken with Provençal Herbs
Boursin Roasted Chicken

Southern Fried Chicken with Cream Gravy

> I think that it was my first job at my cousin Steve's fried chicken business, Mack's Fried Chicken, in Old Algiers, that allowed me to perfect my chicken-frying technique. When it's done well, there is nothing in this world like fried chicken. Lather some cream gravy on top and eat it with Southern Grits (page 162) and perhaps some Collard Greens (page 144) or some of MaMa's Green Beans (page 141), and think about dieting tomorrow.

2 cups all-purpose flour
1½ tablespoons Tony Chachere's Creole Seasoning
1 large egg
1½ cups milk
1 chicken (about 3½ pounds), cut in 8 pieces
4 cups vegetable oil for frying

Gravy

2 tablespoons all-purpose flour
1 small onion, finely chopped
3 scallions, thinly sliced
2½ cups milk
Salt and freshly ground black pepper, to taste

In a large bowl or plastic bag, combine the flour with the Creole seasoning. In a medium bowl, whisk the egg together with the milk.

Coat the chicken pieces with seasoned flour by dredging them on all sides in the bowl or shaking, a few pieces at a time, in the bag. Shake off excess flour, dip the chicken pieces in the eggwash, and then coat again with the seasoned flour. Place the coated chicken on a baking sheet or plate until ready to fry.

Preheat the oven to 200°F.

In a large, deep skillet, heat the oil over medium-high heat until almost smoking. Fry the chicken in the hot oil, turning frequently, until golden brown on all sides and cooked through, 20 to 25 minutes (see Note).

When the chicken is done, remove with a slotted spoon to paper towels to drain, and keep warm in the preheated oven while you make the gravy.

Carefully pour out most of the hot oil from the skillet, leaving the crumbly bits on the bottom. Add the flour to the skillet and cook it, stirring, with the crumbly bits and oil until all is a medium brown color. Add the onion and scallions and sauté until tender, about 5 minutes. Whisk in the milk, little by little, until smooth, and cook until thickened, about 5 minutes. Remove from the heat and season with salt and pepper.

Serve the fried chicken topped with the gravy.

SERVES 4

NOTE: The legs and thighs will take the longest to cook, and are done when they float to the top of the oil. If you find that the chicken is becoming too brown on the outside well before the specified amount of time has passed, reduce the heat. If the chicken gets too brown on the outside before it is cooked through, you can drain it on paper towels and finish cooking it on an ungreased baking sheet in the oven at 300°F.

Chicken and Dumplings

In my opinion, this is one of the most underrated comfort foods I know. MaMa Armstrong always made chicken and dumplings with flat, noodle-like dumplings, so I have a particular fondness for this type of dumpling and have given instructions for these below.

Broth

2 chickens (3½ pounds each), backs removed and cut into 8 pieces
3 tablespoons canola oil
1 large onion, coarsely chopped
6 cups water
2 bay leaves
1 teaspoon salt

Dumplings

2 cups all-purpose flour
4 teaspoons baking powder
1 teaspoon salt
3 tablespoons butter
1 cup milk

5 tablespoons butter
8 tablespoons flour
¼ cup dry white wine
1 teaspoon thyme leaves, crumbled
3 ribs celery, cut into ½-inch pieces on the diagonal
4 carrots, peeled and cut into ½-inch pieces on the diagonal
1 large onion, cut into 1-inch pieces
¼ cup heavy cream
¾ cup frozen peas, thawed
Salt and freshly ground black pepper, to taste
3 tablespoons chopped fresh parsley

Cut chicken backs, necks and wings into 1-inch pieces.

In a large, heavy Dutch oven, heat the oil over medium-high heat. Add the chicken backs, necks, and wings and the chopped onion. Sauté until the chicken is lightly browned, about 5 to 7 minutes. Add the remaining chicken pieces, water, bay leaves, and salt and bring to a boil. Reduce heat to low and simmer, partially covered, until the chicken is tender, about 30 minutes. Remove the chicken pieces and set aside. Discard the chicken backs, necks and wings. When the chicken pieces have cooled, remove the meat from the bones in chunks and set aside. Strain broth and discard the vegetables.

Prepare the dumplings: In a medium bowl, mix the flour, baking powder, and salt together. In a small saucepan over low heat, bring the butter and milk to a simmer. Stir the butter and milk mixture into the dry ingredients with a fork and stir until the mixture just comes together. On a lightly floured surface, roll the dough out into ⅛-inch thickness. Cut into long strips 1-inch wide. Set aside.

In the cleaned Dutch oven, melt the butter over medium heat. Whisk in the flour and cook until golden-brown, 1 to 2 minutes. While whisking, add the wine, the reserved chicken broth, and thyme. Cook until thickened, about 5 minutes, then add the celery, carrots, and onion. Cook until the vegetables are tender-crisp, about 15 minutes. Add the reserved chicken meat, heavy cream, and peas. Season with salt (if necessary), and black pepper to taste.

Place the dumplings on top of chicken mixture and gently stir into the hot liquid. Cover and simmer until dumplings are cooked through, about 10 minutes. Gently stir in the parsley. Serve in large soup bowls.

SERVES 6 TO 8

Chicken and Sausage Gumbo

I remember quite well the first time I ever made gumbo. It was during my college years, shortly after getting my first apartment. It was such a small apartment there was a "½" included in the street address, and was actually part of an old shotgun house in the Spanish Town section of downtown Baton Rouge. I shared the house with my friends Beth and Will, and we had this mutually beneficial arrangement of often having supper together. I decided to get fancy one day and thought I'd impress them with my gumbo, but not actually having any idea what I was doing, I called MaMa Armstrong for instructions. Even so, I was certain I had a fiasco on my hands when I added the roux to the liquid, horrified that I had ruined a whole chicken. That was my first moment of kitchen magic. I stood there and watched the transformation take place. As the liquid warmed up, the brown globules of roux melted into it, and it wasn't long until I had some very decent gumbo on my hands.

I don't make my gumbo exactly like MaMa Armstrong's anymore. Nor like MaMa LaChute's. Gumbo is a signature sort of dish—everyone's tastes different. They can be made with many different things, with or without okra, with or without filé. They are thick, thin, made with a roux or roux-less. This is mine.

Serve it over rice, accompanied by hot sauce and a loaf of hot, crusty French bread to pass around.

Stock

1 chicken, cut into 8 pieces
1 onion, unpeeled, quartered
1 rib celery, cut into 2-inch lengths
2 cloves garlic, smashed with the side of a knife
1 bay leaf

1 cup (2 sticks) butter
1 cup all-purpose flour
3 onions, chopped
2 ribs celery, chopped

½ green bell pepper, seeded and finely chopped
8 cloves garlic, pressed or minced
¾ teaspoon crushed red pepper
2 chicken bouillon cubes
1 to 1½ pounds smoked sausage, such as kielbasa
1 bunch scallions, chopped
⅓ cup chopped parsley
Salt and cayenne pepper, to taste
6 to 8 cups hot, cooked white rice, for serving

Combine the chicken, onion, celery, garlic, and bay leaf in a large pot with enough water to cover and bring to a boil. Lower the heat to a simmer and cook, uncovered, for 45 minutes, skimming frequently. If the water reduces so the chicken is exposed, add more water to cover.

Meanwhile, make a roux by melting the butter in a large, heavy saucepan or cast-iron skillet then whisking in the flour. Cook over medium heat, stirring constantly, until the roux is a chocolate-brown color. This could take from 20 to 40 minutes, depending on the pot you are using as well as the stove. It is important that you stir constantly, otherwise you will burn the roux. At the moment you see the roux beginning to take on a chocolate-brown color, add the chopped onion, celery, bell pepper, and garlic all at once. Stir well to combine and let cook until the vegetables are tender, about 5 to 7 minutes.

If by this time the chicken has simmered for 45 minutes or so, remove from the heat and strain the stock, removing the chicken pieces to a plate and discarding the vegetables. Return the stock to the pot and slowly whisk in the roux-vegetable mixture. Add the crushed red pepper and chicken bouillon cubes and let simmer, uncovered, for 2 hours, stirring occasionally and skimming off any froth or scum that rises to the top.

Once the chicken has cooled enough to handle, debone and remove all skin and cartilage. Set the chicken meat aside, covered, until later.

While the gumbo is simmering, slice the sausage and sauté it in a hot skillet over medium-high heat until browned on both sides. Remove from the heat and add to the gumbo.

After the gumbo has simmered the proper length of time, add the chicken, chopped scallions, and parsley. Stir well to mix and let simmer another 30 minutes. Add salt and cayenne pepper to taste.

Serve in large bowls over hot, cooked white rice.

SERVES 6

Pan-Fried Breast of Chicken with Red-Eye Gravy

This is a simple way to "fry" chicken, much quicker and less caloric than Southern Fried Chicken (page 103). I serve it with grits and red-eye gravy. The red-eye gravy, so named because of the coffee in the recipe, is what makes this dish special. If you are counting calories, you can substitute water for the cream in the gravy and still get good results.

Chicken

1 cup yellow cornmeal
3 whole chicken breasts, split, skinned, and boned
Salt and freshly ground black pepper, to taste
¼ cup canola oil
4 tablespoons butter

Red-Eye Gravy

½ pound ham, cut into ¼-inch cubes
1 bunch scallions, chopped
1 cup strong black coffee
2 cups chicken stock (or 2 cups water plus 1 chicken
    bouillon cube)
¼ cup heavy cream

Southern Grits (page 162)

Preheat the oven to 300°F.

Spread the cornmeal in a shallow bowl. Season chicken breasts with salt and pepper on both sides and then dredge each piece in the cornmeal to coat both sides.

In a large, heavy skillet, heat the oil over high heat. When it is very hot, add the butter. Add the chicken breasts and sauté until golden brown and crispy on both sides, 6 to 8 minutes. Remove the breasts from the skillet and transfer to a baking sheet. Bake the chicken in the oven 5 to 10 minutes, or until cooked through.

While the chicken is baking, make the gravy. Add the cubed ham to the drippings in the skillet and let it brown over medium-high heat for 1 or 2 minutes, stirring. Add the scallions and sauté until tender, about 3 minutes. Add the coffee and chicken stock and let simmer 5 minutes. Add the heavy cream, then taste and adjust the seasoning, if necessary.

Serve the chicken with grits and the gravy.

SERVES 6 TO 8

Chicken Braised with Garlic and Green Olives

Having had a grandfather who made lengthy pilgrimages to any grocery store where he could obtain real Italian or Greek olives, I grew up thinking of them as a daily delicacy. PaPa LaChute was always in search of the consummate olive. Always excited when he found olives superior to the last batch he'd procured, I wonder how he would have reacted had he been with me when I first discovered the luscious, vibrant green olives from Cerignola. They are undoubtedly the most beautiful green olives I have ever seen, about twice the size of most olives, with a subtle, fresh flavor not to be found elsewhere. They inspired this dish, and I think they are well worth a trip to an upscale Italian deli or gourmet food store. However, if you cannot find them, I have also had good results with regular green Spanish olives from a jar.

¼ cup olive oil
2 chickens (about 3½ pounds each), each cut into 8 pieces
    and skin removed
Salt and freshly ground black pepper, to taste
1 large onion, sliced
15 cloves garlic, pressed or minced
1 red bell pepper, seeded and sliced
½ teaspoon crushed red pepper
1½ cups dry white wine
2 tablespoons all-purpose flour
1 can (28 ounces) Italian plum tomatoes, undrained and
    broken up with your hands
2 chicken bouillon cubes
8 ounces green olives, preferably from Cerignola, or
    Spanish olives
Crisped Polenta (page 166)

In a large, heavy saucepan or deep skillet, heat the oil over high heat until hot but not smoking. Season the chicken on both sides with salt and pepper, then brown on both sides in olive oil, 4 to 5 minutes per side. Remove the chicken to a platter and set aside.

Add the onion, garlic, bell pepper, and crushed red pepper to the drippings in the skillet and sauté until the vegetables are tender and beginning to caramelize around the edges, 5 to 7 minutes, stirring frequently. Add the wine and cook until the liquid is almost completely evaporated, 3 to 5 minutes. Dust the vegetables in the skillet with the flour, mix well, and cook 2 to 3 minutes. Add the tomatoes and bouillon cubes and cook until the cubes are dissolved and the mixture is slightly thickened, 5 minutes.

Return the chicken pieces to the skillet and, if necessary, add just enough water to cover the chicken. Add the olives, cover, and reduce the heat so the chicken just simmers. Cook 30 to 45 minutes, until the chicken is very tender.

Meanwhile, preheat the oven to 200°F.

Using a slotted spoon, remove the chicken pieces to an ovenproof bowl and set in the warm oven. If sauce seems too thin, increase the heat and reduce liquid to appropriate thickness. Taste sauce and adjust seasoning, if necessary. Serve the chicken over the polenta, topped with the sauce.

SERVES 6 TO 8

Chicken Pot Pie

I think that chicken pot pie is one of the most underrated comfort foods of all time. What follows is my rendition of this classic. The porcini mushrooms go a long way toward making it something special, and the fresh herbs add a nice, lively touch.

This can be prepared in advance and stored, covered with plastic wrap, in the refrigerator for up to 24 hours, or in the freezer for up to 6 weeks.

Eat while hot and enjoy with a crisp green salad.

Pastry

2 cups unbleached all-purpose flour
1 teaspoon salt
¾ cup (1½ sticks) cold butter, cut into small pieces
1 large egg yolk
¼ cup cold water, or more as needed
1 tablespoon heavy cream, for brushing the dough

Filling

¼ ounce dried porcini mushrooms
1 cup water
4 tablespoons butter
2 whole chicken breasts, split, boned, skinned, and cut into
    1-inch chunks
1 large onion, roughly chopped
1 medium rib celery, sliced or chopped
8 ounces fresh button mushrooms, wiped free of dirt and
    stem ends trimmed
2 cloves garlic, pressed or minced
½ cup dry white wine
4 tablespoons unbleached all-purpose flour
3 cups chicken stock (or 3 cups water plus 1 chicken
    bouillon cube)
¾ cup heavy cream, or more as needed

3 carrots, peeled and sliced on the diagonal
1 baking potato, peeled and cut into ½-inch cubes
3 sprigs fresh thyme
Freshly ground black pepper, to taste
½ cup fresh or frozen green peas
¼ cup chopped fresh parsley
Salt, to taste

Make the pastry: In a medium bowl, combine the flour and salt. Add the butter pieces, and, with a pastry blender, two knives or your fingertips, cut the butter into the dry ingredients until the mixture resembles coarse crumbs. Mix the egg yolk with the ¼ cup water, sprinkle over the flour mixture, and toss with a fork to mix. Knead briefly, only until the pastry comes together. If it seems dry, add a bit more water. Shape into a flattened disk shape and refrigerate, wrapped in plastic, for at least 1 hour, while you prepare the filling.

Quickly rinse the porcini mushrooms under cold running water to get rid of any sand. Place them in a small saucepan with the water and bring to a boil. Let the mushrooms boil for 2 minutes, then remove from the heat and let them steep in the hot water while you proceed with the recipe.

In a large skillet, melt the butter over high heat. Add the chicken and sauté until golden brown on all sides, 7 to 10 minutes. Using a slotted spoon, remove the chicken to a bowl and set aside. Add the onion, celery, and mushrooms to the drippings in the skillet and continue cooking over high heat until the onions are tender and mushrooms are browned and release no more juices, 5 to 7 minutes, stirring frequently. Add the garlic and cook 1 minute, stirring constantly, so the garlic doesn't scorch. Add wine and continue to cook until almost all liquid has evaporated, 2 to 3 minutes, then add the flour, stirring well, and cook 1 to 2 minutes. Add the chicken stock and heavy cream and stir well to mix, cooking until the sauce begins to thicken, about 5 minutes. Strain porcini mushroom liquid through a fine sieve and add to the skillet. Add the carrots, potato, thyme, and black pepper. Stir well, reduce the heat to low, and cook, uncovered, stirring frequently, until the potatoes and carrots are tender, about 15 minutes. Stir in the reserved chicken, peas, parsley, and salt. If the sauce seems too thick, add more water or heavy cream; if it seems thin, continue to cook another few minutes until it has reduced to the desired consistency. Remove from the heat and season with salt. Transfer the mixture to a 2-quart casserole dish and let cool completely.

Preheat the oven to 350°F.

When the filling is completely cooled and the pastry has been refrigerated at least 1 hour, remove the pastry from the refrigerator and roll it out on a lightly floured surface to a thickness of ¼ inch in the shape of the casserole dish you are using. Carefully transfer the pastry to the top of the casserole dish and trim the edges so approximately 1 inch hangs over the sides of the casserole. With your hands, bring the overhanging pastry inside the casserole, folding it under and pressing it decoratively to the sides, sealing the contents within. This needn't be exact and shouldn't be a source of stress—this dish is rustic and will be good no matter how professional the top ends up looking. Cut several vents in the center of the pastry to allow steam to escape. Brush the pastry with the heavy cream.

Bake 35 to 40 minutes, or until the pastry is golden brown and some of the filling is bubbling up out of a steam vent or two.

SERVES 6

NOTE: If the pastry has been in the refrigerator for a long time, you may have to let it sit at room temperature until it becomes pliable enough to roll out.

Roast Chicken with Provençal Herbs

Everyone loves roast chicken, and this version, rubbed with olive oil and garlic and then accented by the wonderful combination of herbs that are found in herbes de Provence, is always met with enthusiasm. I like to add some vegetables to the roasting pan the last 45 minutes of cooking time. They soak up the drippings from the chicken and complete the main course all at once. Potatoes, carrots, fennel, onions, bell peppers, parsnips, and squash can all be thrown in together, for a colorful side dish.

1 chicken (3½ to 4 pounds)
2 tablespoons olive oil
6 cloves garlic, pressed or minced
1½ teaspoons Tony Chachere's Creole Seasoning
Freshly ground black pepper, to taste
1 tablespoon herbes de Provence

Preheat the oven to 450°F.

Rinse the chicken well under cold running water and pat dry with paper towels. Rub the chicken all over with the oil, then pat the garlic on evenly. Season the chicken, inside and out, with the Creole seasoning and a liberal amount of freshly ground black pepper. Sprinkle all over with the herbes de Provence.

Place chicken in a roasting pan, breast side up, and roast for 15 minutes. Turn the chicken over and cook another 15 minutes.

Reduce the oven temperature to 375°F and turn the chicken again, so it is once more breast side up. Continue to roast until the juices run clear, 35 to 40 minutes. Let the chicken stand 5 to 10 minutes before carving.

SERVES 4

Boursin Roasted Chicken

While traveling in the south of France, I was fortunate enough to be invited to dinner at the home of some relatives of a friend, and this is what I was served. It is truly delicious and remarkably easy to make, and no one will ever guess that the secret ingredient and sauce itself is Boursin cheese.

1 chicken (3½ to 4 pounds)
Salt and freshly ground black pepper, to taste
1 tablespoon olive oil
2 packages (5.2 ounces each) Boursin (garlic and fines herbes flavor)

Preheat the oven to 400°F.

Rinse the chicken well under cold running water and pat dry with paper towels. Season the chicken well, inside and out, with salt and pepper. Coat the bottom of a roasting pan or shallow casserole dish with the oil. Place the chicken in the roasting pan and place one whole block of Boursin inside the cavity of the chicken. Break off one-fourth of the second block of Boursin and pat it over the breast of the chicken. Leave the remainder of the second block of Boursin at room temperature while roasting the chicken.

Place the roasting pan in the center of the oven. After about 10 minutes, once the Boursin has softened and begun to melt on top of the chicken, remove the pan from the oven, and using the back of a spoon, spread the Boursin all over the chicken. Return the pan to the oven and roast for 25 minutes, until the chicken is golden brown on top. Remove the pan from the oven and turn the chicken over so the back is now facing up. A small amount of Boursin will probably begin to ooze out of the chicken cavity at this point, so take a bit of it and spread it all over the back side of the chicken. Return the pan to the oven and roast until the back side of the chicken is golden brown, about 25 minutes. Remove the pan from the oven one more time. Reduce the oven temperature to 375°F and turn chicken over again, so the breast is once again facing up. Continue to cook until the chicken is done, 20 to 30 more minutes. Test for doneness by inserting a knife at one thigh joint and seeing that the juices run clear.

When the chicken is done, remove it from the oven and transfer to a platter or cutting board. Set aside, loosely covered with aluminum foil. Carefully remove and discard as much rendered fat from the roasting pan as possible. Add ½ cup hot water and the remainder of the second Boursin to the roasting pan. Remove any remaining melted Boursin from the cavity of the chicken and add to the roasting pan.

Carve the chicken into serving pieces, allowing the juices from the chicken to run onto the platter. Add the juices to the roasting pan and mix well with the Boursin, drippings, and water. Serve the sauce spooned over the chicken pieces.

SERVES 4

Meat

Daddy's Barbecued Beef Brisket
Seared Calves' Liver with Balsamic Vinegar and Red Wine Sauce
Veal Scallops with Artichokes and Lemon-Shiitake Sauce
Sunday Dinner Pork Roast with Mushroom Gravy
Stuffed Pork Tenderloin with Mustard Sauce
Short Ribs with Sweet Potatoes, Dried Fruits, and Indian Spices
Sausage and Chicken Jambalaya
Garlic Roast Leg of Lamb with Rosemary
Rosemary Lamb Shanks

Daddy's Barbecued Beef Brisket

Apparently the love of food and the gift of being able to prepare it well was passed on to my dad from MaMa Armstrong. Like many folks in Louisiana, Daddy works in the oil business, and one of his primary duties at Deltide, the oil tools company he represents, is to host "cookouts" for their clients. Every other week or so, Daddy feeds anywhere from fifty to a hundred hungry men. His barbecued brisket is legendary (really), and the recipe that follows is his original. You may think he's exaggerating when he says in the recipe to cook it until it falls apart, but I guarantee you that is exactly what he means. He insists that unless you need spatulas to pick up the brisket, it's not done enough.

Zatarain's Crab Boil is a Louisiana product that can be found in many seafood markets and gourmet food and spice markets. It has a distinct flavor and should not be substituted for unless absolutely necessary.

1 whole beef brisket (8 to 12 pounds), untrimmed
2 packets (3 ounces each) Zatarain's Crab Boil in a bag
6 tablespoons liquid Zatarain's Crab Boil
1 large onion, quartered
1 medium green bell pepper, seeded and coarsely chopped
3 medium ribs celery, coarsely chopped
1 tablespoon garlic powder
Tony Chachere's Creole Seasoning
1 large bottle Italian Salad Dressing
Your favorite barbecue sauce

Rinse the brisket under cold running water and drain. Place it in a large gumbo pot and cover with water. Add both types of crab boil, the onion, bell pepper, celery, and garlic powder and bring to a boil over high heat. Reduce heat to medium and continue to boil, uncovered, at least 2 to 2½ hours, turning the brisket in the pot every half hour or so and adding water as necessary to keep the brisket covered. Check with a fork for tenderness. The brisket is done when it is impossible to lift it from the pot with a fork without it falling apart. When it is done, remove the brisket from the pot. Daddy says that two spatulas work well here. Scrape off all the fat with a spoon or dull knife.

Prepare the grill.

Season the brisket all over with the Creole seasoning. Grill the brisket, basting continuously with Italian dressing to keep it from drying out, about 10 minutes on each side, then move the brisket to the outer edge of the grill (away from the hot coals) and continue to cook, turning and basting frequently, for another 30 to 45 minutes, depending on how hot the grill is. Do not overcook, or the brisket will be dry.

When the brisket has cooked long enough, cover it with your favorite barbecue sauce and remove it from the grill. Slice it with a very sharp knife (an electric knife works well here), across the grain, and serve immediately.

SERVES 4 TO 6

Seared Calves' Liver with Balsamic Vinegar and Red Wine Sauce

The combination of liver and onions has always been a favorite of mine. This recipe is embellished with some much-reduced dry red wine, and the hint of vinegar gives it an indiscernible undernote that complements the liver very well. Try serving this with Roast Potatoes (page 151), mashed potatoes or even Puréed Sweet Potatoes with Orange (page 153) and a simple vegetable like Sautéed Cucumbers (page 146).

4 cups dry red wine
8 tablespoons butter
2 large red or Spanish onions, thinly sliced
4 sprigs fresh thyme or ½ teaspoon dried thyme, crumbled
2 large shallots, minced
1 cup all-purpose flour
2 tablespoons balsamic vinegar
2½ cups beef stock or canned beef broth
1 cup canned Italian plum tomatoes, drained, seeded, and finely chopped
¼ cup heavy cream
Salt and freshly ground black pepper, to taste
3 pounds calves' liver, very thinly sliced
6 tablespoons canola oil
½ cup chopped parsley, for garnish

In an enameled or other nonreactive medium saucepan, bring the wine to a boil over medium-high heat and continue to boil until it has reduced to ½ cup, about 30 minutes, removing it from the heat when ready and setting it aside.

While the wine is reducing, melt 3 tablespoons of the butter in a large skillet. Add the onions and thyme and sauté over medium-low heat, stirring frequently, until the onions have released all of their juices, are very tender, and have begun to caramelize around the edges, 20 to 25 minutes. Remove from the heat and transfer the onions to a small bowl. Cover to keep warm.

In the same skillet, melt 2 tablespoons of the remaining butter over medium heat. Add the shallots and sauté until tender, about 5 minutes. Whisk in 2 tablespoons of the flour and cook for 1 minute before adding the balsamic vinegar and beef stock. Whisk well to combine and bring to a simmer, still over medium heat. Simmer until thickened, about 10 minutes, stirring occasionally, then add the reduced wine and tomatoes and simmer until ready to serve the liver. Add the heavy cream, then taste and season with salt and pepper.

Season the remaining flour with salt and pepper and spread on a plate. Lightly dredge the liver, one piece at a time, in the seasoned flour to coat on both sides, shaking off excess flour. Place the pieces on a plate as you dredge.

In a large, heavy skillet, heat 2 tablespoons of the canola oil over medium-high heat until very hot, then add 1 of the remaining tablespoons of butter and then one-third of the liver. Sauté the liver quickly, only 2 to 3 minutes per side for medium-rare. Repeat procedure until all liver has been sautéed, wiping out skillet between batches.

Transfer the liver to a platter and serve immediately, topped with the caramelized onions and red wine sauce and garnished with the chopped parsley.

SERVES 6

Veal Scallops with Artichokes and Lemon-Shiitake Sauce

Marinated artichoke hearts add an interesting note to this otherwise-classic pairing of flavors. This dish is not only delicious, but simple to put together and can be prepared in no time at all. I recommend serving the veal over pasta or roasted potatoes, with a simple green vegetable such as asparagus, broccoli, or snow peas.

5 tablespoons butter
1 large onion, finely chopped
½ red bell pepper, seeded and finely chopped
2 cloves garlic, pressed or minced
¾ cup all-purpose flour
1½ cups water
2 chicken bouillon cubes
1 cup heavy cream
Grated zest and juice of ½ lemon
2 jars (6½ ounces each) marinated artichoke hearts, drained
    but 3 tablespoons of the marinade reserved
¼ teaspoon crushed red pepper
8 ounces fresh shiitake mushrooms
2 scallions, thinly sliced on the diagonal
Salt and freshly ground black pepper, to taste
8 very thin scallops of veal (about 1½ pounds)
3 tablespoons canola oil

In a medium saucepan, melt 2 tablespoons of the butter over medium heat. Add the onion, bell pepper, and garlic and sauté until tender, about 5 minutes. Add 3 tablespoons of the flour, stir well to mix, and cook for 1 minute. Slowly whisk in the water, bouillon cubes, and heavy cream and cook until the bouillon cubes are dissolved and the mixture has thickened, about 10 minutes, stirring occasionally. Reduce the heat to low and add the lemon zest, lemon juice, marinated artichoke hearts, the 3 tablespoons reserved artichoke marinade, and crushed red pepper and continue to cook for 10 to 15 minutes, until the flavors have come together and the sauce is of a pleasing consistency. Remove from the heat and keep warm.

In a large skillet, melt 1½ tablespoons of the remaining butter over medium-high heat. Add the shiitake mushrooms and sauté until tender and golden brown around the edges, 4 to 5 minutes. Remove from the heat and add to the sauce, along with the scallions. Remove from the heat, stir well to mix, and season with salt and pepper.

Season the remaining flour with salt and pepper and spread on a plate. Lightly dredge the veal scallops, one at a time in the flour to coat on both sides, shaking off excess flour. Place the scallops on a plate as you dredge.

In the same skillet used for the mushrooms, heat the canola oil over high heat, and when hot but not smoking, add the remaining 1½ tablespoons butter then the veal. Sauté the veal quickly until golden on both sides—this should only take 1 to 2 minutes per side. Do not overcook the veal.

Transfer the veal to a platter and serve immediately, with the sauce spooned on top.

SERVES 4

Sunday Dinner Pork Roast with Mushroom Gravy

Sunday "dinner" after church was usually at MaMa Armstrong's, and a pork roast often had the starring role. This was accompanied by hot rice and gravy, Collard or Turnip Greens (page 144) or MaMa's Green Beans (page 141), and Smothered Squash (page 157). The recipe has been updated a bit from MaMa's, but one thing remains: you must cook the roast for much longer than you would ever think necessary. In the South, a roast isn't done unless it is, literally, falling apart. Corn Pudding with Caramelized Onions (page 145) would also be great here.

Pork

1 pork roast, such as loin or butt (5 to 7 pounds)
1 whole head garlic, cloves separated and peeled
Louisiana Red Hot, as needed
1 tablespoon Tony Chachere's Creole Seasoning
1 teaspoon garlic powder
3 tablespoons canola oil
1 large onion, chopped
2 medium ribs celery, chopped
½ medium green bell pepper, seeded and chopped
2 tablespoons teriyaki sauce
1 teaspoon Worcestershire sauce

Mushroom Gravy

6 tablespoons butter
4 tablespoons all-purpose flour
1 medium onion, finely chopped
½ medium green bell pepper, seeded and finely chopped
1 medium rib celery, finely chopped
2 cloves garlic, pressed or minced
½ bunch scallions, tops separated from bottoms, both chopped

2 cups beef stock or canned broth (or 2 cups water and 1
    beef bouillon cube)
½ cup heavy cream
1 pound fresh button mushrooms
2 tablespoons teriyaki sauce
½ teaspoon Kitchen Bouquet
Salt and freshly ground black pepper, to taste

Cooked white rice or mashed potatoes, for serving

Preheat the oven to 450°F.

Pierce the roast all over with a paring knife and stuff one clove of garlic into each hole with a few drops of Louisiana Red Hot, then sprinkle the roast all over with the Creole seasoning and garlic powder. Heat the oil in a large skillet or roasting pan over medium-high heat. Add the roast and brown it on all sides, 10 to 15 minutes, then remove to a large casserole or Dutch oven and sprinkle with the chopped onion, celery, and bell pepper. Pour in enough water to come 1 inch up the sides of the casserole. Add the teriyaki sauce and the Worcestershire sauce.

Roast the pork, covered, for 45 minutes, then reduce the oven temperature to 350°F (adding more water if the level has reduced) and continue to cook, still covered, until the roast is very tender, about 3½ hours.

While the roast is cooking, make the gravy. Melt 4 tablespoons of the butter in a medium saucepan, then whisk in the flour. Cook over medium heat, stirring constantly, until the roux is a medium brown color, about 10 minutes. Add the onion, bell pepper, celery, garlic, and the white part of the chopped scallions. Continue to cook, stirring occasionally, until vegetables are tender, about 5 minutes. Whisk in the beef stock and heavy cream and cook until thickened, 10 to 15 minutes.

While the sauce is simmering, heat the remaining 2 tablespoons butter in a medium skillet over medium-high heat. Add the mushrooms and sauté until tender and golden brown around the edges, 4 to 5 minutes. Remove from the heat and add to the gravy along with the teriyaki sauce and the Kitchen Bouquet.

When the roast is done, remove it from the casserole to a platter and cover loosely with foil to keep warm. Strain cooking juices through a sieve, pressing on the solids to extract as much liquid as possible. Discarding the solids, stir the cooking juices into the gravy in the skillet and simmer until thickened, 10 minutes. Remove from the heat and season with salt and pepper.

Slice the roast with a very sharp knife or an electric knife and serve with the gravy over cooked rice or mashed potatoes.

SERVES 4 TO 6

Stuffed Pork Tenderloin with Mustard Sauce

Pork tenderloin, with its low fat content, makes a wonderful meat to serve meat lovers who are also concerned about eating healthily. I like it for this reason, but also for the facts that it is quick and simple to prepare, and unless you overcook it, it is always moist and tender. In the recipe that follows, I have stuffed the tenderloins with a traditional Cajun stuffing and then topped it with a sauce flavored by one of pork's greatest flavor enhancers, mustard. I like to serve this with rice (although Southern Grits, page 162, or Creamy Polenta, page 165, would also be great here) and simple vegetables, such as Sautéed Cucumbers (page 146) or Collard Greens (page 144).

Stuffing

1 tablespoon butter
2 tablespoons canola oil
3 medium ribs celery, finely chopped
1 medium green bell pepper, seeded and finely chopped
1 large onion, finely chopped
4 scallions, finely chopped
1½ teaspoons dried thyme, crumbled
1 teaspoon Tony Chachere's Creole Seasoning
¼ teaspoon freshly ground black pepper

2 pork tenderloins (about 1 pound each), trimmed of all fat
Salt and freshly ground black pepper, to taste
¼ cup unseasoned dry bread crumbs

Sauce

½ cup of reserved stuffing from above
1 tablespoon all-purpose flour
2 tablespoons whole-grain Dijon mustard
1⅓ cups water

⅔ cup heavy cream
1 chicken bouillon cube
Salt and freshly ground black pepper, to taste

Cooked white rice, for serving

Prepare the stuffing. In a large skillet, heat the butter and canola oil over medium heat. Stir in the remaining stuffing ingredients and sauté until the vegetables are tender, 6 to 8 minutes, stirring frequently. Remove from the heat, taste and adjust the seasoning if necessary, and let cool to room temperature before proceeding. Set aside ½ cup of the stuffing for the sauce.

Preheat the broiler.

Season the tenderloins all over with salt and pepper. Make a lengthwise cut, ¾ to 1 inch deep, down the top center of each tenderloin, to create a channel into which the stuffing will fit. Loosely pack the cooled stuffing into the channels on top of the tenderloins, then sprinkle the tenderloins with the bread crumbs.

Broil tenderloins approximately 4 inches away from the heat source about 12 to 15 minutes, or until an instant-reading meat thermometer inserted into the meat reads 150°F.

While the tenderloin is broiling, make the sauce. Heat the reserved ½ cup stuffing in a skillet over medium-high heat, stirring, then dust with the flour and cook, stirring for 2 minutes. Stir in the mustard. Whisk in the water and heavy cream, along with the bouillon cube, and cook until the bouillon cube is dissolved and the mixture has thickened, about 10 minutes, stirring occasionally. Remove from the heat and season with salt and pepper.

When tenderloins are ready, remove them from the broiler to a platter and let stand, loosely covered with foil, 5 minutes before slicing. Serve, with the sauce, over cooked rice.

SERVES 4

Short Ribs with Sweet Potatoes, Dried Fruits, and Indian Spices

It may seem an unlikely combination, but the savory and spicy mingle quite well with the sweet and fruity in this dish. Another great make-ahead dish, this is a complete entrée when served with basmati rice or couscous, and the flavor actually improves over time.

4 ounces dried apricots
4 ounces pitted dried prunes
2 cups dry white wine
¼ cup canola oil
6 pounds beef short ribs
Salt and freshly ground black pepper, to taste
1 pound carrots, peeled and cut into ½-inch slices
4 medium ribs celery, sliced
2 medium onions, coarsely chopped
10 cloves garlic
5 tablespoons chopped peeled fresh ginger
2 teaspoons ground cinnamon
1 teaspoon ground allspice
½ teaspoon ground cloves
2 teaspoons ground cumin
½ teaspoon ground coriander
1 teaspoon crushed red pepper
2 cups apple cider
4 cups beef or chicken stock (or 4 cups water plus 2 beef or
    chicken bouillon cubes)
2 cups water
½ cup heavy cream
3 large sweet potatoes, peeled and cut into 8 wedges each
4 parsnips, peeled and cut into ½-inch slices
1 bunch fresh cilantro, leaves only, chopped
Cooked basmati rice, for serving
½ cup sliced almonds, lightly toasted, for garnish

In a small, enameled or other nonreactive saucepan, combine the dried fruits with the white wine and bring to a boil over medium heat. Cook until fruit has softened and plumped a bit, about 5 to 10 minutes, then remove from the heat and set aside.

In a large, heavy stovetop casserole or Dutch oven, heat the oil over high heat until almost smoking. Add the short ribs and brown very well on all sides. Remove the ribs from the casserole with a slotted spoon and set aside.

Add the carrots, celery, and onions to the drippings in the casserole and sauté, still over high heat, until tender and beginning to caramelize around the edges, 7 to 10 minutes, stirring occasionally. Add the garlic and ginger and cook another 2 to 3 minutes, stirring constantly, so the garlic and ginger don't scorch.

Add the cinnamon, allspice, cloves, cumin, coriander, and crushed red pepper. Stir well and cook a few minutes to allow the spices to release their perfume.

Remove the dried fruits from the wine with a slotted spoon and set aside. Add the wine to the casserole, scraping any browned bits from the bottom, and cook until the liquid has reduced by a third, 4 to 5 minutes. Add the cider, stock, and water to the casserole, along with the short ribs, and bring to a boil. Cover the casserole and lower the heat so the contents just simmer. Cook until short ribs are almost tender, 1 to 1½ hours.

Remove from the heat and transfer the short ribs from the casserole to a bowl. Set aside, lightly covered. Skim off any fat that has risen to the surface of the cooking liquid.

In a food processor or blender, purée the cooking liquid, in batches, until smooth. Return it to the casserole, along with the short ribs, heavy cream, sweet potatoes, and parsnips. Cook until short ribs and vegetables are tender, 20 to 25 minutes. Add the reserved poached fruits and simmer 10 minutes. Stir in the cilantro. Remove from the heat, and taste and adjust the seasoning, if necessary.

Serve over cooked basmati rice and garnish with the toasted almonds.

SERVES 6

Sausage and Chicken Jambalaya

If you want an easy, one-dish meal for a crowd, this is it. Jambalaya is akin to gumbo in that everyone makes it differently. It is important to remember when you are seasoning the broth that you are also seasoning for all the rice you will be adding, so slight overseasoning is a must. Serve with a green salad and a loaf of crusty French bread.

3 tablespoons canola oil
1 chicken (3½ to 4 pounds), cut in 8 pieces
1 whole chicken breast, split
1½ pounds smoked sausage, such as kielbasa, cut
    into ½-inch dice
2 large onions, finely chopped
4 medium ribs celery, finely chopped
1 green bell pepper, seeded and finely chopped
1 bunch scallions, tops separated from bottoms, both
    chopped
6 cloves garlic, pressed or minced
¼ cup tomato paste
1 can (4 ounces) chopped green chilies, drained
1 teaspoon dried thyme, crumbled
1 bay leaf
1 teaspoon salt, or to taste
Generous amount of freshly ground black pepper, to taste
½ teaspoon crushed red pepper flakes
½ teaspoon Tabasco or other hot pepper sauce
1½ teaspoons Tony Chachere's Creole Seasoning
2 chicken bouillon cubes
5 cups water
1½ cups chopped fresh tomatoes
3 cups long-grain rice
½ cup chopped fresh parsley

In a very large, heavy Dutch oven or stovetop casserole, heat the oil over high heat. Add the chicken pieces, including the breasts, and sauté until browned on all sides, 3 to 4 minutes per side. You will probably have to do this in two batches. Using a slotted spoon, remove the chicken to a bowl and set aside. Add the sausage to the drippings in the Dutch oven, reduce the heat to medium-high, and sauté, stirring, until the sausage is browned on all sides, 4 to 5 minutes. Remove the sausage with the slotted spoon to the bowl with the chicken. Add the onions, celery, bell pepper, chopped scallion bottoms, and garlic and sauté over medium heat until vegetables are tender, about 5 minutes. Return the chicken and sausage to the Dutch oven, along with the tomato paste, canned chilies, thyme, bay leaf, salt, pepper, crushed red pepper, Tabasco, Tony Chachere's Creole Seasoning, bouillon cubes, water, and tomatoes and bring this to a simmer, stirring well to mix. Cover, reduce the heat to low, and cook for 45 minutes, or until the chicken is very tender and the broth has absorbed the flavors of the sausage and seasonings.

Increase the heat to high and add the rice and chopped green scallion tops. Stir well and bring to a boil. Immediately reduce the heat to low and simmer, covered, for about 20 minutes, until the rice is cooked and has absorbed all the liquid. Remove from the heat, and taste and adjust the seasoning, if necessary. Remove the bay leaf and stir in the parsley. Let stand 10 to 15 minutes, covered, before serving.

SERVES 8 TO 10

Garlic Roast Leg of Lamb with Rosemary

For lamb lovers, this is perhaps the quintessential cut of meat. I prefer leaving the bone in, as it gives the meat much more flavor than it would have otherwise. Make sure to leave a sliver of fat on the side that will be up during roasting: This serves as a sort of self-basting technique. With the garlic and rosemary paste, nothing more need be done to the meat to ensure its heavenliness. I think the perfect accompaniments are Ratatouille (page 154) and Goat Cheese Mashed Potatoes (page 150), and I love to preface this meal with Salade de Susan et Philippe (page 189).

1 leg of lamb (bone in) (6½ pounds)
1 whole head garlic, cloves separated and pressed or minced
6 tablespoons finely chopped fresh rosemary
⅓ cup extra-virgin olive oil
1 tablespoon kosher salt
2 teaspoons freshly ground black pepper

Preheat the oven to 450°F.

Trim the excess fat from the leg of lamb, leaving a thin layer on the outer, fattier side of the leg.

Combine the remaining ingredients and mash into a thick paste, using either a mortar and pestle or the side of a knife against a cutting board.

Place the leg of lamb in a shallow roasting pan, fatty side up, and spread the garlic-rosemary paste all over it (see Note). Place the pan in the preheated oven and reduce the heat to 350°F. Cook for about 1 hour 15 minutes for medium-rare, or until a meat thermometer inserted in the thickest part of the meat, away from the bone, registers 145° to 150°F.

Remove from the oven. Transfer the lamb to a platter and let stand, loosely covered with foil, 10 to 15 minutes before carving.

SERVES 6 TO 8

NOTE: If you have extra fresh rosemary, it is nice to roast lamb directly on top of a bed of the sprigs.

Rosemary Lamb Shanks

Rosemary and lamb is simply one of those consummate combinations that can't be challenged. I like to serve shanks at dinner parties when I particularly want to impress my guests: They make such a grand entrée, with each person feeling as if they have their own personal roast of sorts.

Note that the shanks can be prepared well ahead of time and refrigerated or frozen until ready to serve. Caution should be taken when re-heating them, however, and this should be done in a heavy saucepan over very low heat to prevent scorching the thick gravy and to ensure that the shanks are heated through.

6 lamb shanks (about ¾ pound each)
Salt and freshly ground black pepper, to taste
¼ cup canola or olive oil
2 large onions, chopped
2 medium ribs celery, finely chopped
2 medium carrots, peeled and finely chopped or grated
8 cloves garlic
1½ cups dry red wine
¼ cup all-purpose flour
4 cups beef or veal stock (or 4 cups water plus 2 beef
    bouillon cubes), or more as needed
¼ cup tomato paste
1 can (28 or 35 ounces) Italian tomatoes, undrained and
    crushed with your hands
3 or 4 large sprigs fresh rosemary or 2 teaspoons dried,
    crumbled
2 sprigs fresh thyme or ½ teaspoon dried, crumbled
½ teaspoon crushed red pepper
1 bay leaf
½ cup chopped fresh parsley
½ cup chopped fresh basil (optional)

Season the lamb shanks well with salt and pepper. Heat the oil in a large saucepan or Dutch oven over high heat. Add the shanks and brown on all sides, 5 minutes per side. Remove shanks from pot and set aside.

Add the onions, celery, carrots, and garlic and sauté over medium-high heat until vegetables are tender and golden around the edges, 7 to 10 minutes, stirring frequently.

Add the wine and cook until reduced by half, about 8 minutes. Add the flour and mix well.

Add the beef or veal stock, tomato paste, tomatoes, rosemary, thyme, crushed red pepper and bay leaf and stir well. Return the shanks to the pot, adding stock or water to cover if shanks are not completely submerged in the cooking liquid. Bring to a boil, skimming off any scum or fat that rises to the top, then reduce the heat to low. Cover and simmer the shanks until very tender, usually 1½ to 2 hours. Uncover occasionally to stir, making sure that nothing is sticking or burning on the bottom of the pot.

Toward the end of the cooking time, preheat the oven to 200°F.

When the shanks are tender (check with a fork—the meat should pull away very easily), remove them to a serving platter or bowl, cover loosely with foil, and keep warm in the oven while you finish the gravy.

Remove the herb stems and bay leaf from the cooking liquid. Remove 1½ to 2 cups of cooking liquid with vegetables to a food processor or blender and purée. Return to the pan, and if the sauce seems too thin, increase the heat so the liquid will reduce to the desired thickness. Remove from the heat and add chopped parsley (and basil, if desired), then taste and adjust the seasoning. Pour the gravy over the shanks to serve.

SERVES 6

Succulent Sides

Growing up in the South as I did, where the number of side dishes present on any table usually well outnumbers all else that is there, has certainly left its mark on me. Not only do side dishes get more than their share of the billing, but they also tend to be "serious" dishes, not merely steamed or boiled vegetables and plain white rice. This also has clearly colored my perception of what a good side dish should be. Here are some recipes that are the perfect complements to selected entrées in this book. I have also included some others that I simply adore too much to leave out.

I have a sneaky suspicion that there are many of you out there who, like me, would be happy to make a meal around side dishes, and the recipes I've included lend themselves well to mixing and matching. Go to it!

Vegetables

MaMa Armstrong's Green Beans
White Bean Au Gratin
Collard Greens
Corn Pudding with Caramelized Onions
Sautéed Cucumbers
Braised Fennel with Parmesan and Cream
Stewed Okra and Tomatoes
Goat Cheese Mashed Potatoes
Roast Potatoes
Aunt Cindy's Sweet Potato Casserole
Puréed Sweet Potatoes with Orange
Ratatouille
Creamed Spinach
Smothered Squash
Stewed Turnips

MaMa Armstrong's Green Beans

I could eat bowls and bowls of these. In fact, I could skip all the other stuff and just gorge myself on green beans, they are that good. MaMa made these all the time, no matter what the menu. Don't try it with fancy French haricots verts, as the green beans have to be able to stand up to a long cooking time—time enough for the flavors of the bacon and onion to meld with that of the beans. These are a must with Sunday Dinner Pork Roast with Mushroom Gravy (page 127).

4 slices bacon
1 medium onion, finely chopped
1½ pounds fresh green beans, ends trimmed
Salt and freshly ground black pepper, to taste
Optional: Sometimes I can't resist adding 1 or 2 cloves of
    smashed garlic to the cooking liquid

In a large saucepan, cook bacon over medium heat until it has rendered most of its fat and has begun to brown, about 5 minutes. Add chopped onion and sauté until translucent, about 5 minutes. Add the green beans and enough water to cover, bring to a boil, and then reduce heat to low. Season with salt and pepper, then cover the saucepan and simmer until the beans are quite tender, about 1 hour, occasionally adding liquid if necessary to cover the beans. As they get close to being done they will become quite fragile, so take care when stirring not to break them apart. Taste and adjust the seasoning, if necessary.

SERVES 4 TO 6

White Bean Au Gratin

Creamy, well-seasoned beans topped with a crispy, flavorful crust—this is the perfect complement to Garlic Roast Leg of Lamb with Rosemary (page 136), Rosemary Lamb Shanks (page 137) or Roast Chicken with Provençal Herbs (page 117), especially alongside Ratatouille (page 154). If you like, you can add an additional clove or two of minced garlic at the end when you stir in the parsley for a more assertive garlic flavor. The beans can be prepared ahead of time up to the point of broiling, then baked instead of broiled, until heated through and top is golden brown and crispy (about 45 minutes). If you opt to prepare the beans ahead of time, leave them a little soupier than you would normally to account for the fact that beans absorb liquid as they sit.

1 pound dried cannellini or Great Northern beans
6 tablespoons olive oil
2 large onions, chopped
2 medium ribs celery, chopped
6 cloves garlic, pressed or minced
1 bay leaf
1 teaspoon dried thyme, crumbled
Freshly ground black pepper, to taste
½ teaspoon crushed red pepper
6 cups unsalted chicken stock (or 6 cups water and 2 chicken
    bouillon cubes) added *after* beans have become tender
Water, if needed
Salt, to taste
½ cup chopped fresh parsley
½ cup unseasoned dry bread crumbs
½ cup grated Gruyère cheese
½ cup grated Parmigiano-Reggiano cheese

Rinse and pick over the beans. Place in a large saucepan and add enough water to cover by 2 inches. Bring to a boil over high heat and cook for 2 minutes, then cover and remove from the heat. Let stand, covered, for at least 1 hour.

In a large flameproof casserole or Dutch oven, heat 3 tablespoons of the oil over medium-high heat. Add the onions, celery, and garlic and sauté until tender and beginning to caramelize around the edges, about 10 minutes. Drain the beans and add them to the casserole along with the bay leaf, thyme, black and red peppers, and chicken stock or 6 cups water and bring to a boil. Cover the casserole and reduce the heat to a simmer. Cook until the beans are very tender, from 1 to 3 hours, depending on the beans used. If 6 cups water was used instead of chicken stock, add the 2 bouillon cubes when the beans are tender. Add water if the beans begin to dry out—there should be some liquid left when the beans are done (see Note). Season with salt and stir in the parsley.

Transfer the beans to a large, shallow gratin dish. Combine the bread crumbs with the grated cheeses and sprinkle over the beans. Drizzle with the remaining 3 tablespoons oil and broil until the top is crispy and golden brown, 4 to 5 minutes.

SERVES 8

NOTE: If the beans are very soupy at the end, remove the casserole cover and increase heat to high and allow liquid to reduce to desired thickness. If you like your beans creamy, mash some against the side of the pot with the back of a spoon.

Collard Greens

Whether greens are prepared for a Cajun or a southern table, they are cooked pretty much about the same: Some sort of smoked or salted meat is added to give them flavor, and they are always cooked to be tender, never crispy! Collards are my favorite, next to turnip greens, with mustard greens coming in third. You can substitute any of the greens that I've mentioned if you can't put your hands on any collards. I've even had success with kale prepared this way.

1 tablespoon canola oil
1 ham hock, skin slit in several places with a sharp knife, or
    8 ounces bacon, salt pork, or fatback
1 large onion, roughly chopped
5 cloves garlic, smashed against a cutting board with the side
    of a knife and peeled
8 cups chicken stock or water
½ teaspoon crushed red pepper
3 to 4 pounds collard greens, rinsed, stems removed, and cut
    into strips crosswise (usually 3 large bunches or so)
1 teaspoon Tony Chachere's Creole Seasoning
Salt and freshly ground black pepper, to taste

In a large saucepan or kettle, heat the oil over medium-high heat. Add the meat and onion and sauté until the meat begins to render some of its fat and juices and onion becomes tender, 5 to 7 minutes. Add the garlic cloves and cook 2 or 3 more minutes before adding stock or water, red pepper and greens. Stir until the greens wilt and become well combined with seasonings. Reduce heat to low and simmer, uncovered, until tender, 45 minutes to 1 hour. Remove from the heat, and taste and adjust the seasoning.

SERVES 6

Corn Pudding with Caramelized Onions

Corn lovers, take note: This is a not-to-be-missed corn extravaganza. Though the recipe calls for and is certainly best when made with fresh corn when it's in season, I have also had excellent results using frozen sweet corn. Sort of a cross between a custard and a soufflé, this is a great dish to serve alongside baked ham or roast poultry, and is a perfect complement to Daddy's Barbecued Beef Brisket (page 121).

3 tablespoons butter
2 medium onions, 1½ thinly sliced and ½ finely chopped
3 large eggs
1 tablespoon cornmeal
1 cup heavy cream
½ cup milk
6 to 8 ears fresh corn, husked and kernels cut from the cob
    (about 3 cups)
½ bunch scallions, finely chopped
¼ teaspoon freshly grated nutmeg
Salt and freshly ground black pepper, to taste

Preheat the oven to 350°F. Butter an 8-inch square casserole or 2-quart soufflé dish with ½ tablespoon of the butter and set aside.

In a large skillet, melt the remaining 2½ tablespoons butter over medium heat. Add the sliced onions and sauté until tender and beginning to caramelize, 10 to 15 minutes, stirring frequently and adding a bit of water if the onions begin to brown before they have softened. Remove from the heat and set aside.

In a large bowl, whisk together the eggs, cornmeal, cream, and milk. Stir in the remaining ingredients, including the finely chopped onion, and pour the mixture into the prepared casserole. Top with the caramelized onions and bake on the middle rack of the oven for 40 minutes, or until the pudding is set and golden brown on top. Serve immediately.

SERVES 6

Sautéed Cucumbers

If you have ever had sautéed cucumbers you will understand why I feel the way I do about them. Exceedingly simple, there is something about the crisp texture of just-sautéed cucumbers, done in real butter, that is indescribably delicious. I love serving them alongside sautéed fish—they're perfect with salmon—but I also like them with roast beef or pork, or even alongside a juicy steak. This is a dish that cannot be made in advance, as cucumbers will wilt and become watery if left to sit once they have been cooked.

6 tablespoons butter
6 medium cucumbers, peeled, seeded, and cut into
    ½-inch slices
Salt and freshly ground black pepper, to taste

In a very large skillet, melt the butter over high heat. Add the cucumbers and sauté 2 to 3 minutes, shaking the pan often to assure even browning. This is a very quick process, and it is of the utmost importance that you do this over as high a heat as possible, locking in the juices of the cucumbers and just searing the outer edges. The cucumbers are done when golden brown around the edges. Season with salt and pepper and serve immediately.

SERVES 4 TO 6

Braised Fennel with Parmesan and Cream

I think that fennel is a vegetable too often overlooked here in America. Perhaps we're just not quite sure what to do with it. While traveling in Italy and the south of France, I saw that it is a chameleon of sorts, changing its character dramatically depending on the method of preparation. A truly refreshing addition to a salad simply sliced raw, it can also add intriguing flavor to seafood stews or serve as an elegant side dish or first course when prepared as I describe below. If you are already familiar with fennel, I know you'll like it prepared this way. If you're naive to its power to delight, perhaps this dish will make a disciple out of you.

3 large fennel bulbs
2 cups chicken stock (or 2 cups water plus 1 chicken
    bouillon cube)
3 cloves garlic, smashed on a cutting board with the side of a
    knife and peeled
Salt and freshly ground black pepper, to taste
1 tablespoon cornstarch
⅓ cup heavy cream
½ cup grated Gruyère cheese
1 cup finely grated Parmigiano-Reggiano cheese

Preheat the oven to 350°F.

Trim the fennel and cut lengthwise into ⅜-inch slices. Layer the slices on the bottom of a large baking dish or casserole, and pour chicken stock over slices. Add the smashed garlic cloves and season with salt and pepper. Cover tightly with foil and bake for 15 minutes. Remove from the oven and turn the slices over, so that any sides that were not immersed in stock during the first 15 minutes are now so. Cover again with foil, return to the oven, and continue to cook another 15 minutes.

Remove from the oven and heat the broiler. By this time the fennel should be tender. (If not, return it to the oven for a short time.) Mix the cornstarch and heavy cream until smooth and pour it over the fennel and stock. Move the slices around a bit to make sure the cream mixture mixes well with the stock, then top with the grated Gruyère and Parmigiano-Reggiano and return to the oven, uncovered, until bubbly and sauce has thickened. Place under the broiler 2 to 3 minutes, or until golden brown on top. Serve with some of the sauce spooned onto the plate.

SERVES 6 AS A SIDE DISH OR 4 AS A FIRST COURSE

Stewed Okra and Tomatoes

Okra is a remarkably versatile vegetable, equally delicious fried, pickled, stewed, or used as a thickener in soups or gumbos. This is one of my favorite ways to have it and, I think, is perhaps the least off-putting for those who may be shy around the fuzzy skin and slimy juices that are more apparent when it is prepared other ways. This is a great accompaniment to fried chicken and grits.

When choosing okra, search out the smaller pieces, as they are more tender, and avoid okra that has brown spots, evidence that the okra has been lying around for a while. Fresh okra is bright green and feels heavy in your hand.

4 slices bacon
1 large onion, coarsely chopped
2 cloves garlic, peeled and smashed against a cutting board
    with the side of a knife
2 packages (10 ounces each) frozen okra, whole or cut, or
    1½ pounds fresh okra, stem ends trimmed, left whole or
    cut into 1-inch pieces
1 can (28 or 35 ounces) Italian plum tomatoes, undrained
    and coarsely chopped
1 teaspoon sugar
1 bay leaf
Seasoned salt and crushed red pepper, to taste

In a large saucepan or skillet, cook the bacon over medium heat until it has rendered its fat, about 5 minutes, then remove the bacon and save for another purpose. Add the onion and garlic to the grease in the skillet and sauté until very tender, about 10 minutes. Add the okra, canned tomatoes with their juices, and the sugar. Add the bay leaf, salt, and crushed red pepper and simmer, uncovered, stirring frequently, until most liquid has evaporated and the okra is no longer "slimy," about 1 hour. Remove the bay leaf before serving.

SERVES 4 TO 6

Goat Cheese Mashed Potatoes

Mashed potatoes may be the ultimate comfort food, and the addition of goat cheese and scallions bring it to new heights. This is a great backdrop for lamb of any sort, and can also be made up to 1 day in advance and then reheated in a microwave or regular oven at the last minute. I find the microwave to be the best way to reheat mashed potatoes—just make sure you stir them several times during the heating process so the heat is evenly distributed. Also, mashed potatoes prepared in advance tend to get a little stiff as they sit—simply add a bit more milk or water when you reheat them, if needed.

5 pounds Idaho or Yukon Gold potatoes, peeled and
    cut into eighths
8 tablespoons (1 stick) butter
1½ cups milk
½ cup heavy cream
½ cup sour cream
Salt and freshly ground black pepper, to taste
12 ounces mild goat cheese, such as Montrachet, crumbled
½ bunch scallions, minced
2 tablespoons finely chopped fresh herb of choice (optional)

In a large saucepan, bring the potatoes to a boil with just enough salted water to cover them. Reduce the heat to a high simmer and cook, uncovered, until the potatoes are quite fork-tender, about 20 minutes. Drain the potatoes in a colander.

In the same saucepan, combine the butter, milk, and heavy cream and heat over low heat until the butter has melted and the milk is simmering. Return the potatoes to the pan and mash with a hand-held masher until the potatoes are smooth. Add the sour cream, salt, pepper, crumbled goat cheese, and scallions and stir well to mix. If you are opting to add fresh herbs, stir them in now. Cover the pot and keep the potatoes hot over very low heat until ready to serve.

SERVES 6

Roast Potatoes

> This is a simple way to roast potatoes and yet end up with beautiful golden-brown rounds of potatoes that look nice on a plate or serve easily as little platforms for grilled or sautéed meat, fish, or chicken.

4 baking potatoes, such as Idaho
2 to 4 tablespoons canola or olive oil, or as needed
1½ teaspoons Tony Chachere's Creole Seasoning

Preheat the oven to 400°F.

Scrub the potatoes well under cold running water, pat thoroughly dry, and cut crosswise into ¼-inch slices.

Pour 2 tablespoons oil on a large, heavy baking sheet and make sure the entire surface is coated evenly. Arrange the potato slices on the baking sheet in a single layer. Sprinkle with the Creole seasoning, then turn the potatoes over, so both sides are coated with oil. Drizzle more oil on the potatoes, if necessary, and bake for 15 to 20 minutes, until the potatoes begin to brown on the bottom. Remove the baking sheet from the oven and turn the potatoes over, using a metal spatula or tongs. Return to the oven until both sides are evenly browned and crispy, about 10 minutes more.

SERVES 6

Aunt Cindy's Sweet Potato Casserole

Well, thank goodness for Aunt Cindy. Because of her, we have this wonderful alternative to the usual marshmallow-topped sweet potato casserole. Needless to say, it's great for Thanksgiving, but also works well with roast chicken or pork. I have even known those who have enjoyed it in place of dessert!

8 medium sweet potatoes, boiled with skins on until just
    fork-tender
8 tablespoons (1 stick) butter, softened
4 large eggs
⅔ cup evaporated milk
1½ cups granulated sugar
2 tablespoons vanilla extract

Topping
8 tablespoons (1 stick) butter, melted
2 cups (packed) brown sugar
⅔ cup all-purpose flour
2 cups chopped pecans

Preheat the oven to 350°F. Grease a 9- × 13-inch baking dish or 3½-quart casserole.

Peel the sweet potatoes, cut into large pieces, and place in the prepared casserole dish. In a medium bowl, whisk together the softened butter, eggs, evaporated milk, granulated sugar, and vanilla until smooth. Pour over the sweet potatoes.

Mix the topping ingredients well and distribute evenly over the sweet potatoes. Bake for 35 to 45 minutes, or until crispy and lightly browned on top.

SERVES 8 TO 10

Puréed Sweet Potatoes with Orange

This is one of my favorite ways to enjoy sweet potatoes, and undoubtedly the simplest. Unlike regular potatoes, which turn to glue if you try to purée them in a food processor, sweet potatoes become silken when just enough liquid is added to purée them. If you are counting calories, they are almost as delicious without the cream and butter and just a little more orange juice. Sweet potatoes prepared this way are a wonderful complement to roasted pork, duck, or chicken, and the consistency is to die for.

These can be made up to 1 day ahead of time and then reheated in a microwave oven.

4 pounds sweet potatoes
4 tablespoons butter
⅓ cup freshly squeezed orange juice
1 teaspoon freshly squeezed lemon juice
¼ cup heavy cream
¼ cup (packed) brown sugar (optional)
1 teaspoon salt, or to taste
Finely grated zest of 1 orange (optional)

Peel the sweet potatoes and cut into 2-inch pieces. Place in a large saucepan with enough water just to cover and bring to a boil over high heat. Cook until the potatoes are very tender, 20 to 30 minutes. Drain in a colander, reserving some of the cooking liquid.

Place the potatoes in a food processor with all the remaining ingredients and process, in batches if necessary, until very smooth, wiping down the sides of the processor bowl several times during processing to ensure a completely smooth purée. If potatoes seem too thick, add a bit of the reserved cooking liquid until the desired consistency is reached.

Serve immediately, or refrigerate, covered, for up to 24 hours. Reheat in the microwave.

SERVES 6

Ratatouille

Saying its name alone is almost as enjoyable as consuming this delectable mélange of vegetables. This is a dish that just begs for Garlic Roast Leg of Lamb with Rosemary (page 136) and Goat Cheese Mashed Potatoes (page 150). If you really want it to be outrageous, you can't skimp on the olive oil or the garlic. Cooking the vegetables separately is also key, and, if possible, make this a day in advance. Giving the vegetables a day to mingle their flavors truly does them justice. Ratatouille made in advance should be cooled then stored in the refrigerator in a nonreactive bowl or casserole dish, covered with plastic wrap.

1 large eggplant, peeled and cut into 1-inch chunks
2 to 3 medium zucchini, cut crosswise into ½-inch slices
1 teaspoon kosher salt
8 tablespoons olive oil, plus more if needed
2 large onions, cut into 1-inch chunks
2 medium bell peppers, red or green or one of each, seeded
    and cut into 1½-inch pieces
10 cloves garlic, pressed or minced
1 can (28 or 35 ounces) Italian plum tomatoes, undrained
    and coarsely chopped
Salt and crushed red pepper, to taste
½ cup chopped fresh basil

Place the eggplant and zucchini in separate stainless-steel or glass bowls and toss each with ½ teaspoon of the salt. Let stand 30 minutes.

Drain the eggplant and then pat thoroughly dry with paper towels. Heat 3 tablespoons oil in a large skillet over medium-high heat. Add the eggplant, one layer at a time, and sauté in olive oil until lightly browned on all sides, 4 to 5 minutes, adding more oil as necessary. Remove to a large bowl or casserole and then do the same with the zucchini. In the same skillet, using 2 tablespoons oil sauté the onions and peppers until tender, 4 to 6 minutes. Stir in the garlic and continue to cook for 1 to 2 minutes, stirring constantly so the garlic won't scorch. Add the tomatoes and season with salt and crushed red pepper. Let simmer for 10 minutes or so, then add the reserved eggplant and zucchini. Continue to simmer until any extra liquid has evaporated and the flavors have had a chance to mingle, 15 to 20 minutes. Stir in the chopped basil, taste and correct the seasoning, if necessary. Let sit for at least 10 minutes, covered, before serving, to give the basil time to release its essence. Serve hot or at room temperature (see Note).

SERVES 6

NOTE: If you do choose to make this a day ahead of time, make sure you reheat slowly, preferably in an enameled casserole in the oven, to prevent scorching the vegetables.

Creamed Spinach

I could just about bury myself in a puddle of this, it's so good, and most people who have tried it feel the same. It's one of my standard Thanksgiving side dishes but also finds good company with a just-seared steak.

4 packages (10 ounces each) frozen chopped spinach (get a
    quality brand, like Birds Eye)
6 tablespoons butter
2 medium onions, finely chopped
6 cloves garlic, pressed or minced
1½ teaspoons dried thyme, crumbled
6 tablespoons all-purpose flour
4 cups heavy cream
Salt and freshly ground black pepper, to taste

Prepare the spinach according to package directions. Drain and squeeze out all excess water, then set aside.

Melt the butter in a large skillet or heavy saucepan over medium heat. Add the onion and garlic and sauté until onion is translucent and very soft, 6 to 8 minutes. If garlic begins to scorch, reduce the heat. Add the thyme and flour and stir well to mix. Continue to cook 1 to 2 minutes, stirring constantly so as not to scorch the flour. Whisk in the cream and cook until the sauce begins to thicken, about 5 minutes. Add the spinach, stirring well, and cook over medium-low heat until the desired consistency is reached. Season with salt and pepper and serve (see Note).

SERVES 8 GENEROUSLY

NOTE: This can be prepared 1 or 2 days in advance, cooled, then refrigerated or frozen until ready to use. Reheat it in a casserole dish in the oven, uncovered, or microwave it until hot and bubbly.

Smothered Squash

Just who came up with the idea of cooking squash for as long as this dish requires, and then deciding to call it something as potentially frightening as "smothered," I could not say. But what I can tell you is that when MaMa Armstrong would tell us that we were going to be privy to smothered squash on a particular day, the announcement was always met with squeals of delight and anticipation. You might have to be the brave sort to try this: After such a long time of cooking, any color the squash had to begin with is long gone, and the appearance is nothing to brag about. One taste, however, is all I think you will need to understand its appeal. It goes very well with Sunday Dinner Pork Roast with Mushroom Gravy (page 127) or Stuffed Pork Tenderloin with Mustard Sauce (page 130).

6 to 8 medium pattypan squash (about 4 pounds), unpeeled
    and cut into 1-inch pieces
4 slices bacon
1 large onion, finely chopped
Salt and freshly ground black pepper, to taste

Bring a saucepan of salted water to a simmer over medium-high heat. Add the squash and simmer until soft, about 15 minutes. Drain and set aside.

In a large, heavy skillet, cook bacon over medium heat until it has rendered its fat, about 6 minutes. Remove the bacon and save for another purpose. Add the onion to the grease in the skillet and sauté until it is very tender, about 8 minutes. Add the squash and salt and pepper. Cook the squash over medium heat, mashing it as it cooks with a potato masher or a fork, until the squash has completely fallen apart and there are no recognizable pieces, about 45 minutes. You will need to stir it fairly often, more so toward the end of cooking, as it tends to scorch on the bottom as the moisture evaporates and the squash breaks down. When the squash is very tender and all excess liquid has evaporated, remove from the heat, season with salt and freshly ground black pepper.

SERVES 6

Stewed Turnips

Turnips are one of those vegetables that many folks shy away from, but I am here to tell you that, when I serve them cooked this way, I have seen the birth of many believers. The sugar cuts the bitter, "turnipy" taste that some find objectionable, and the bacon just does what it always does. I love turnips this way with Sunday Dinner Pork Roast with Mushroom Gravy (page 127).

2 slices bacon
3 pounds small white turnips, peeled and cut crosswise into
    ½-inch slices
½ cup sugar, plus more if needed
Salt and freshly ground black pepper, to taste

In a large saucepan, cook the bacon over medium heat until it has rendered its fat and begun to take on a little color, about 6 minutes. Add the sliced turnips along with the ½ cup sugar and enough water to cover. Season with salt and pepper, then cover and simmer until the turnips are tender. This could take from 25 minutes to an hour, depending on the turnips you've chosen. If at the end of the cooking time the turnips have any bitterness left to them, add a bit more sugar. Serve hot.

SERVES 6

Breads and Other Grains

Perfect Biscuits

Don't think that I label these biscuits "perfect" lightly. A result of endless researching and testing, this recipe makes biscuits that are buttery and crispy on the outside, light and flaky on the inside, with no yeasty after-taste. Serve them piping hot from the oven with lots of butter.

2½ cups all-purpose flour
2 tablespoons sugar
1½ teaspoons baking powder
½ teaspoon salt
½ teaspoon baking soda
6 tablespoons butter
Scant 1 teaspoon dry quick-rise yeast
1½ tablespoons warm water
1 cup buttermilk
2 tablespoons melted butter, for brushing the biscuit tops

Preheat the oven to 400°F.

In a large bowl, sift together the flour, sugar, baking powder, salt, and baking soda. Using a pastry blender, two knives, or your fingertips, cut in the 6 tablespoons butter until the mixture resembles coarse crumbs.

In a small bowl, dissolve the yeast in the warm water. Add the yeast mixture and buttermilk to flour mixture, stirring only until just incorporated. Do not overwork the dough.

Place the dough on a lightly floured work surface, sprinkle with a bit of flour, and roll out to a thickness of ¾ inch. Cut the dough into biscuits with a 2-inch cookie cutter, or with the rim of a glass that has been dipped in flour, and place on an ungreased baking sheet. Brush with the melted butter and bake 10 to 15 minutes, until risen and golden brown.

MAKES ABOUT 1½ DOZEN 2-INCH BISCUITS

Corn Bread

This corn bread is an amalgamation of many recipes I've tried, and I think I finally hit the nail on the head. If you want corn bread that is crispy on the outside, use a cast-iron skillet and heat it in the oven. When you are ready to bake the corn bread, remove the skillet from the oven and add butter to the skillet, quickly twirling to coat the sides and bottom, then add the batter and bake immediately.

2 to 3 tablespoons butter for greasing the baking pan
1 cup yellow stone-ground cornmeal
1 cup all-purpose flour
2 teaspoons baking powder
¼ teaspoon baking soda
1 teaspoon salt
2 large eggs
1 cup canned cream-style corn
½ cup sour cream
½ cup buttermilk
½ cup vegetable oil
2 jalapeños, seeded and minced (wear gloves please!)
2 scallions, finely chopped

Preheat the oven to 375°F and grease a 9-inch square baking pan (or skillet, as described above) with the butter.

In a large bowl, combine all the dry ingredients. In another bowl, whisk together all the remaining ingredients until smooth. Add to the dry ingredients, stirring just until combined.

Transfer the batter to the prepared baking pan or skillet and bake in the middle of the oven for 35 to 45 minutes, until lightly browned on the top and a toothpick inserted in the center comes out clean. Transfer to a cooking rack and let the corn bread cool in the pan for 5 minutes before slicing. Serve hot.

SERVES 4 TO 6

Southern Grits

I have always loved grits, but I had to travel to Charleston, South Carolina, to get a tip on how to make them truly irresistible. While vacationing there once, I had a memorable meal at Louis's Charleston Grill. I had the opportunity to ask about the grits, and was told that they'd been made with cream. I came up with the following recipe as an approximation of the grits I experienced there. If you are on a fat-restricted diet, simply decrease the amount of cream and replace it with an equivalent amount of milk, skim milk, or water.

Before we begin, I must tell you that you can't rush grits. Like polenta, they simply must cook for a certain length of time well after they may look or seem done. Don't attempt to save time by using instant grits, as so much of the true flavor and texture of grits has been stripped away in order to make them cook so quickly. Also, a heavy pot is indispensable for grits, as they become quite thick and will undoubtedly scorch on the bottom during the cooking process in a thin pot.

If you find yourself with any leftover grits, don't throw them out! You will see that as they cool, they become firm, and can be sliced and sautéed in butter, creating quite a different beast altogether. In this way, grits carry over well from the breakfast table straight through to dinner, and make an unusual starch substitute for those times when potatoes or rice seem passé.

Salt, to taste
6 cups water
1½ cups grits (old-fashioned or quick cooking, *but not instant*)
2 cups milk
1 cup heavy cream
8 tablespoons (1 stick) butter
½ bunch scallions (optional), sliced
Freshly ground black pepper, to taste

In a large, heavy saucepan, bring 6 cups of salted water to a rapid boil over high heat. Stir in the grits all at once and mix well. As soon as the grits begin to thicken, add the milk, cream, and butter. Reduce the heat to low, cover, and cook 45 minutes to an hour, uncovering frequently to stir (see Note). When the grits are done, they will not be the least bit crunchy in your mouth, only smooth and creamy. Add the scallions, if desired, 5 to 10 minutes before the end of the cooking time. Taste and season with salt and pepper, then serve immediately.

SERVES 6

NOTE: It is important to cook the grits over as low a heat as possible and have the pot covered. You may need to add a bit of water if the grits get too thick. This will depend on the kind of grits you use as well as how tightly the cover fits on your pot.

Cheddar and Scallion Grits

Just a bit more sinful than the preceding recipe. There is something about the combination of cheese and grits that begs to be eaten with bacon, ham, Southern Fried Chicken with Cream Gravy (page 103) or Pan-Fried Breast of Chicken with Red-Eye Gravy (page 110).

Salt, to taste
6 cups water
1½ cups grits (old-fashioned or quick cooking *but not instant*)
2 cups milk
1 cup heavy cream
8 tablespoons (1 stick) butter
1½ cups grated Cheddar cheese
1 bunch of scallions, tops only, chopped finely
Freshly ground black pepper, to taste

In a large, heavy saucepan, bring salted water to a rapid boil over high heat. Stir in the grits all at once and mix well. As soon as the grits begin to thicken, add the milk, cream, and butter. Reduce the heat to low, cover, and cook 45 minutes to an hour, uncovering frequently to stir (see Note page 163). When the grits are done they will not be the least bit crunchy in your mouth, only smooth and creamy. Add the cheese and scallions in the last 10 minutes of cooking time. Taste and season with salt and pepper, then serve immediately.

SERVES 6

Creamy Polenta

I like to think of polenta as Italy's answer to grits. Having lived for years in fear of preparing polenta (many cookbooks make it seem so difficult), once I realized how similar it is to grits, and that the cooking process is almost identical, I began to include it in my repertoire more and more. Like grits, polenta can be prepared very simply, using only water and salt, but you can also make something good into something fabulous by being a little naughty and throwing in a bit of cream, cream cheese or mascarpone, butter, grated cheese, etc. . . . Get the idea?

Salt, to taste
5 cups water
1 cup stone-ground yellow cornmeal
¼ cup heavy cream
4 ounces cream cheese or mascarpone, at room temperature
2 tablespoons butter or olive oil
Freshly ground black pepper, to taste
Milk or water, if needed
½ cup finely grated Parmigiano-Reggiano cheese

In a large, heavy saucepan, bring 5 cups of salted water to a rolling boil. Whisking constantly, pour the cornmeal into the water in a steady stream until all is combined. Continue to whisk until you are sure there are no lumps of unincorporated cornmeal. Reduce the heat to low, cover, and cook 20 minutes, uncovering frequently to stir.

Stir in the heavy cream, cream cheese, and butter and continue to cook, covered, another 20 minutes or so, stirring often. When the polenta is smooth, with no taste of rawness, add salt and pepper to taste (add a bit of milk or water if the polenta seems too thick) and serve, garnished with the grated cheese.

SERVES 6

Crisped Polenta

If you need a starch with a bit of texture to it, try this. I like to use polenta prepared this way as a sort of pillow for something else, such as Chicken Braised with Garlic and Green Olives (page 112), or Rosemary Lamb Shanks (page 137), anything with a sauce that can be swept up by a forkful of polenta. Or, for a simple but elegant side dish or first course, try topping a portion of Crisped Polenta with a few tablespoons of garlic-infused olive oil, perhaps some sautéed shiitake or portobello mushrooms, and then garnish with some grated Parmigiano-Reggiano.

Care should be taken when sautéing the polenta that the skillet and olive oil or butter be very hot when you add the polenta, otherwise it will stick to the pan. I find this works best if you use a skillet with a nonstick finish and don't move the polenta around at all while it is sautéing. Simply let it cook until crisp without any attention whatsoever (save not to let it burn).

Salt, to taste
4 cups water
1 cup stone-ground yellow cornmeal
¼ cup heavy cream
4 ounces cream cheese or mascarpone, at room temperature
8 to 10 tablespoons butter or olive oil
Salt and freshly ground black pepper, to taste
Finely grated Parmigiano-Reggiano cheese, for garnish
   (optional)

In a large, heavy saucepan, bring 4 cups of salted water to a rolling boil. Whisking constantly, pour the cornmeal into the water in a steady stream until all is combined. Continue to whisk until you are sure there are no lumps of unincorporated cornmeal. Reduce the heat to low, cover, and cook 20 minutes, uncovering frequently to stir.

Stir in the heavy cream, cream cheese, and 2 tablespoons of the butter, and continue to cook, covered, another 20 minutes or so, stirring often. When the polenta is smooth, with no taste of rawness, add salt and pepper to taste. Pour the polenta into a large, greased baking pan with sides, or into two greased pie plates, and allow to cool completely. This can be done up to 1 day in advance and refrigerated, covered.

When you are ready to serve the polenta, turn the pan or pie plates over on top of a cutting board or counter. The polenta should fall right out. Cut the polenta into squares or wedges of appropriate serving size. Heat the remaining 6 to 8 tablespoons butter in a nonstick skillet over high heat. Add the polenta and sauté until golden brown and crispy around the edges, 2 to 3 minutes. Carefully flip the pieces to the other side and do the same. When both sides are crispy and golden brown, it is ready and should be served immediately. Garnish with finely grated Parmigiano-Reggiano, if desired.

SERVES 6 TO 8 AS A SIDE DISH OR 4 TO 6 AS A FIRST COURSE

Salad Sense

There are no hard and fast rules about salads. They can be amazingly stimulating at the beginning of a meal, remarkably digestive at meal's end, or meals in and of themselves. Most simply, salads are good for us, providing we don't go crazy with the dressings.

The salads that follow are varied, some light and refreshing and some substantial enough to be eaten as main courses, if desired. Many of them work quite well as accompaniments to specific entrées, and I have noted this in the recipes.

The most important thing to remember about salads is that their simple nature dictates that everything that goes into one must be of the utmost freshness and quality. Vegetables should be firm and vividly colored, and possess a pleasing fresh scent. Greens should never be spotty or wilted. If less than fresh is all you can find, skip it. The nutritional value will undoubtedly be compromised, not to mention the taste. Have something else instead, and wait for a better salad day to arrive.

I also want to urge experimentation among the salad-timid. Today is the day of the gourmet market and "superstore" grocery stores. These stores regularly stock a wide array of lettuces and beautiful, sometimes exotic produce, so we really have no excuse for not trying some of these newly available products. Some of the lettuces I am particularly fond of are lollo rossa and red oak, both of which are beautifully colored and possess amiable flavors and textures that add interest to a simple green salad; Bibb, for the tender sweetness of its small inner leaves; mâche, also known as lamb's lettuce, for its tiny leaves; and frisée, for its bitter taste and dramatic appearance.

Think color, taste, and texture.

Salads

MaMa's Green Bean Salad
Fusilli and White Bean Salad
Fresh Beet and Onion Salad
Warm Chicken Salad with Apples, Walnuts, and Gorgonzola
Miss Myrtle's Coleslaw
Corn and Black Bean Salad
Couscous Salad
Cucumber Salad
Johanna's Greek Salad
Mrs. Burlette's Lobster Salad
Asian Noodle Salad with Sesame-Soy Vinaigrette
Aunt Retta's Potato Salad
My Potato Salad
Salade de Susan et Philippe
MaMa's Shrimp Salad
Spinach Salad with Warm Bacon Vinaigrette
Lentil Salad
Basmati and Wild Rice Salad with Dried Fruits and
Toasted Walnuts

MaMa's Green Bean Salad

There were several ways I could tell summer had arrived in New Orleans—temperature and humidity often matched, with numbers near 100. The quiet hum of air conditioners hard at work would descend upon the city, and most signs of life were to be found indoors, in retreat from the unrelenting heat. The exception was my Uncle Bud, who lived down the River Road from MaMa LaChute. He could often be seen making a pilgrimage down to MaMa's, arms full of whatever extra his garden had given him. In the summer it was usually green beans, and this is my version of what MaMa would do with them.

> 1½ pounds fresh green beans or haricots verts, ends
>   trimmed
> 1 medium red onion, thinly sliced
> 4 large eggs, hard-cooked, peeled, and thinly sliced
>
> Vinaigrette
>
> 2 teaspoons Dijon mustard
> ¼ cup red wine vinegar
> 1½ teaspoons salt, or to taste
> ¾ to 1 cup canola oil
> Freshly ground black pepper, to taste

Fill a large, heavy saucepan almost full with salted water and bring to a boil. Add the green beans all at once and blanch just until they are tender-crisp, about 5 minutes. The length of time this will take will depend on the type and toughness of green beans you are using. Just keep checking.

When the beans are done, transfer them with a slotted spoon to a bowl of ice water to stop the cooking. When the beans have cooled, remove them from the water and let drain in a colander.

Meanwhile, make the vinaigrette. In a large stainless-steel or glass bowl, whisk together the mustard, vinegar, and salt. As you whisk, add the oil in a thin, steady stream until emulsified. You may not need all of the oil, depending on the acidity of the vinegar you are using. Season with pepper.

Arrange the drained beans in a large shallow bowl or serving dish and scatter the sliced onion on top. Arrange the egg slices on top of the onion slices and pour the vinaigrette over all. The salad can be served immediately, or it can marinate in the vinaigrette, covered with plastic wrap and refrigerated, for up to 1 hour.

SERVES 6

Fusilli and White Bean Salad

Though simple can be best, when it comes to pasta salads I can never control my urge to throw a little of everything into one. What follows is my favorite combination of tastes and textures—I love the way the beans get a little creamy and soak up the oil and vinegar, and the occasional bursts of flavor provided by the sun-dried tomatoes and Kalamata olives. The savory flavor of the prosciutto actually makes this salad substantial enough to serve as a main course for a light luncheon or early summer dinner.

1 pound dried fusilli
½ medium red onion, finely minced
1 medium red bell pepper, seeded and thinly sliced
2 medium carrots, peeled and coarsely grated
3 cloves garlic, finely pressed or minced
½ cup sun-dried tomatoes in olive oil (about 8 pieces), drained and roughly chopped
4 ounces Kalamata olives, pitted and roughly chopped or halved
4 to 6 very thin slices prosciutto, finely chopped or torn
¼ cup balsamic vinegar
¼ cup red wine vinegar
½ cup extra-virgin olive oil
¼ cup canola oil
½ cup finely grated Parmigiano-Reggiano cheese
½ cup finely chopped fresh basil
4 scallions, thinly sliced on the diagonal
½ teaspoon crushed red pepper
1 teaspoon salt, or to taste
Freshly ground black pepper, to taste
1 can (15 ounces) white beans (cannellini), rinsed well and drained

In a large saucepan, bring 5 quarts of salted water to a boil. Add the pasta and return to a boil, stirring occasionally. Cook, stirring occasionally, until al dente, 9 to 11 minutes. In a colander drain the pasta. Rinse cooked pasta under cold running water and allow to drain again, thoroughly. Place the pasta in a very large bowl and add all the remaining ingredients except the beans. Mix thoroughly, then gently fold in the beans. Let the salad sit for at least 45 minutes and up to 1 day, refrigerated, for flavors to develop. Check seasoning, and for best results, let the salad return to room temperature before serving.

SERVES 6 TO 8

Fresh Beet and Onion Salad

Why do beets get such a bad rap? Is it because of initial introductions to the canned variety? The color? The mess they make, the stains they leave wherever they've been? I love them. Have always loved them. Even canned. Love to stare at their beautiful concentric ring patterns. Love the feeling of my fork going through them when cooked just enough. Love the fact that they're so good for me. Love this salad, which is a fresh beet version of a canned beet salad my mom used to make.

When choosing fresh beets, I find that small ones are best—they are less likely to be tough and fibrous. Choose beets of uniform size so that they all cook at the same rate. Also, it is important not to overcook beets. Test for doneness by inserting a narrow knife blade into one of the beets. The knife should go in with some resistance—if the knife plummets in, the beets are overcooked. After being cooked, you will find that usually their skins will just rub off. A paring knife can help out if the skin seems to be sticking.

A practical note: I find it useful to keep a few pairs of plastic gloves in the kitchen for jobs that are exceedingly messy or caustic (such as hot peppers), and peeling beets definitely fits the definition here. Surgical gloves work especially well, as their thinness allows you to retain dexterity and control over your movements. If you don't have gloves, don't despair: Though it appears that it will last for days, beet juice will actually wash off with just a few hand washings. Unfortunately, it seems to stain countertops and clothing, so I always make it a point to tackle this task inside a large bowl or over the kitchen sink.

3 pounds fresh beets
1 teaspoon salt
½ cup cider vinegar
Freshly ground black pepper, to taste
½ teaspoon ground allspice
1 pinch ground cloves
3 tablespoons sugar
1 teaspoon Dijon mustard

¼ cup canola oil
1 red onion, thinly sliced
Finely sliced scallion greens or snipped chives, for garnish

Trim the greens from the beets, leaving ½ inch of stems so as not to cut into the flesh of the beets. In a saucepan just large enough to hold the beets, cover the beets with cold water. Add 1 teaspoon of salt to the water and bring to a boil. Cook until just tender-crisp. The amount of time this will take depends on the size beets you've chosen, but start checking after 10 minutes. Remove the beets from the water and allow to cool slightly, then refrigerate, uncovered, to chill, at least 1 hour.

In a medium stainless-steel or glass bowl, whisk together all the remaining ingredients except the red onion. Add the onion and toss to coat with the dressing, then set aside until the beets are chilled.

When the beets are chilled, peel and cut into ¼-inch crosswise slices. Arrange in a shallow glass bowl or on individual salad plates. Arrange the marinated sliced onions on top of beets, making sure to spoon some of the vinaigrette onto each serving, and garnish with sliced scallions. Serve immediately.

SERVES 4 TO 6

Warm Chicken Salad with Apples, Walnuts, and Gorgonzola

A sort of variation on the classic Waldorf salad, this is a lighter, crunchier version that works well as a light luncheon entrée. If all you're in the market for is a great apple salad, simply omit the chicken breasts and use less of the dressing. Though I have been found hunting voraciously for leftovers of this in the fridge the next day, it is at its absolute best the day it's made.

2 whole chicken breasts, split, skinned, boned, and cut into
    1-inch cubes
¾ teaspoon dried thyme, crumbled
½ teaspoon Tony Chachere's Creole Seasoning
2 tablespoons canola oil
5 medium red apples, such as Gala or MacIntosh, peeled
    and cubed
6 medium ribs celery, diced
1½ cups walnuts, lightly toasted
¾ pound Gorgonzola, crumbled
¾ cup raisins

Vinaigrette

½ cup plus 2 tablespoons cider vinegar
1½ teaspoons salt
3 tablespoons sugar
1 teaspoon Worcestershire sauce
¼ cup freshly squeezed lemon juice
¾ cup canola oil
Freshly ground black pepper, to taste

Boston or Bibb lettuce leaves, for serving

Sprinkle the cubed chicken on all sides with thyme and Creole Seasoning. In a large skillet, heat the oil over high heat until hot but not smoking. Add the chicken and sauté until golden brown on all sides and cooked through, 4 to 5 minutes. Remove the chicken with a slotted spoon to paper towels to drain and cool slightly.

In a large bowl, combine the apples with the celery, walnuts, Gorgonzola, raisins, and warm chicken. In a small bowl or lidded jar, combine the ingredients for the vinaigrette and whisk or shake well to blend. Pour over the apple and chicken mixture and toss thoroughly to coat. Check seasoning and serve immediately, on top of Boston or Bibb lettuce leaves.

SERVES 8

Miss Myrtle's Coleslaw

It is a common thing in New Orleans for people to get together for fish fries, much like barbecues (we do that, too!). I used to accompany my Armstrong grandparents to their friends Myrtle and Garland's on such occasions. Coleslaw was an integral part of such a gathering, and I always thought Miss Myrtle's coleslaw recipe was special. I now realize that it is the lack of mayonnaise that makes it unusual, being light and crunchy instead of rich and cloying. Given that it takes a seat next to fried foods, it seems a good thing to skip the mayo here. If creamy is a must for your coleslaw, however, you can add ½ cup of mayonnaise after the salad has marinated overnight and still get good results.

1 cup cider or distilled white vinegar
1⅓ cups sugar
1 teaspoon celery seed
1 teaspoon mustard seed
2 cups diced celery
1 medium green bell pepper, seeded and finely chopped
1 large onion, finely chopped
2½ to 3 pounds cabbage, shredded (about 10 cups)
3 to 4 medium carrots, peeled and grated (about 1 cup)
Salt and freshly ground black pepper, to taste

In a small enameled or other nonreactive saucepan, heat the vinegar and sugar over medium heat, stirring, until hot and the sugar is completely dissolved. Remove from the heat.

In a very large stainless-steel or glass bowl, combine the remaining ingredients and pour the hot vinegar mixture over all. Toss well to coat, then cover with plastic wrap and place in the refrigerator. Marinate overnight, stirring occasionally.

When ready to serve, taste and season with salt and pepper.

MAKES 2 QUARTS OR MORE, SERVING 8 GENEROUSLY

Corn and Black Bean Salad

Though I know little of the Zen concept of yin and yang, I would bet that the classic combination of corn and black beans must exemplify the ideal of this philosophy. It is a perfect marriage of textures and flavors, and I love making a salad, or sort of salsa, out of the combination. It is difficult to mess this salad up—one reason I like to make it often, in any number of guises. It is of course best when made with fresh, tender summer corn, but in winter frozen corn and canned beans can make people happy, too. My favorite way to serve it is with grilled or sautéed salmon and roast potatoes. Be sure to taste and adjust the seasoning just before serving, as the salad will usually need more salt, especially if you have opted to include tomatoes, which tend to release their juices after being seasoned.

3 cups cooked fresh corn kernels (about 6 ears), cooked, or
    2 packages (12 ounces each) frozen corn kernels, thawed
4 cups cooked or 2 cans (15 ounces each) black beans, rinsed
    and drained
1 medium red bell pepper, seeded and finely chopped
2 medium tomatoes, seeded and coarsely chopped (optional)
1 small red onion, finely chopped
5 scallions, thinly sliced
1 jalapeño pepper, seeded and finely minced (optional, wear
    gloves please!)
½ cup chopped fresh cilantro

Vinaigrette
¼ cup red wine vinegar
Juice of ½ lemon
Juice of ½ lime
½ cup canola or olive oil, or a combination of the two
1½ teaspoons salt, or to taste (see Note)
Freshly ground black pepper, to taste

In a large stainless-steel or glass bowl, combine the corn, beans, bell pepper, tomatoes, onion, scallions, jalapeño if using, and cilantro. In a lidded jar, combine the ingredients for the vinaigrette and shake well to blend. Pour over the corn and bean mixture and toss gently but thoroughly, taking care not to crush the beans.

Allow the salad to stand 45 minutes to 1 hour at room temperature for the flavors to come together. Taste and adjust the seasoning just before serving.

SERVES 6

NOTE: The amount of salt you will need will vary depending on the acidity of the vinegar and lemon and lime juice you use.

Couscous Salad

There is something fun about eating couscous, little tiny spheres of pasta that take to any sort of seasoning imaginable. I like to follow the Asian tendency of balancing sweet with savory, thus the raisins and choice of spices in this salad. It makes a great accompaniment to grilled chicken or lamb.

This is one of those add-what-you-like dishes. Fresh tomatoes, chickpeas, or oil-cured black olives are among the additions I sometimes make.

2 ¼ cups water
1 teaspoon salt
1 tablespoon olive oil
1 package (10 ounces) couscous
3 medium carrots, peeled and coarsely grated
½ medium red bell pepper, seeded and finely minced
2 medium ribs celery, sliced thinly on the diagonal
1 small red onion, finely minced
1 sweet apple, such as Golden Delicious or Gala, cored and cut into ½-inch dice
1 medium cucumber, peeled, seeded, and chopped
½ cup golden raisins
3 scallions, thinly sliced (about ⅓ cup)
½ cup finely chopped fresh parsley

Dressing

⅓ cup fresh lemon juice
⅓ cup olive oil
Salt, to taste
¼ teaspoon cayenne pepper
½ teaspoon ground cinnamon
½ teaspoon ground allspice
½ teaspoon ground cumin

In a medium saucepan bring the water, salt, and oil to a boil over medium-high heat. Add the couscous and stir well to mix. Cover immediately and remove from the heat. Let stand 5 minutes, then toss gently with a fork. Let cool completely, tossing occasionally to ensure even cooling.

Combine the cooled couscous in a large stainless-steel or glass bowl with the carrots, bell pepper, celery, onion, apple, cucumber, raisins, scallions, and parsley. In a lidded jar, combine the ingredients for the dressing and shake well to blend. Pour over the couscous mixture and toss thoroughly to coat. Taste and adjust the seasoning, if necessary. Let stand 30 minutes at room temperature before serving.

SERVES 4 TO 6

Cucumber Salad

Perhaps I would have loved cucumbers in any case, but as it is I have such nice memories of my PaPa LaChute and his garden, where cucumbers always flourished, that I couldn't not love cucumbers if I tried. PaPa LaChute was a man of few words and often communicated through food. If you were offered something from his hands you truly felt you were special in his eyes.

I think that the simplest and best way to really appreciate a cucumber is how PaPa used to—icy cold from the fridge, with just a little salt sprinkled on it. However, if you have to get a bit more complicated, try this salad. PaPa probably would have cursed me in French for having to do this to a cucumber to enjoy it, but then that would have been just fine with me. His curses almost always came with a smile and were definitely reserved for those whom he loved.

8 large cucumbers, peeled, seeded, and thinly sliced
1 onion, peeled and thinly sliced (optional)
1 tablespoon salt
¾ cup sugar
¾ cup distilled white or cider vinegar
Salt and freshly ground black pepper, to taste

Place the sliced cucumbers and onions in a colander and sprinkle with salt. Stir to distribute the salt evenly and let stand for 1 hour, stirring occasionally. (Place the colander over a bowl to drain.)

Rinse the cucumbers quickly under cold water and then squeeze them with your hands to remove any extra water. Place the cucumbers and onions if using in a large stainless-steel or glass bowl and add all the remaining ingredients. Stir well to mix, then refrigerate, covered, until well chilled, about 1 hour.

Before serving stir well and adjust the seasoning.

SERVES 4 TO 6

Johanna's Greek Salad

I have a friend who has a husband, an ex-husband, a son named Maximilian, and a recipe for the best Greek salad I've ever eaten. It is left over from the first husband, who was Greek, and from what I understand is perhaps the best thing that came from that union. It by no means can compete whatsoever with the fruit of her marriage today, for little Max is an angel incarnate. But if you're in the market for a truly exceptional, truly traditional Greek salad, try this one.

Johanna says that traditionally this salad is eaten communally, with just one big bowl in the middle of the table and everyone dipping and dunking pieces of bread as the spirit moves them. If you're not feeling quite so intimately acquainted with your dining partners, individual salad bowls work quite well. Don't forget to dunk your bread—the juice left in the bottom of the bowl is the most heavenly part of this experience.

1 medium onion, quartered lengthwise and sliced crosswise
8 ounces fine-quality Greek or Bulgarian feta cheese, in water
1 cup fine-quality extra-virgin olive oil
2 teaspoons dried oregano, Greek if possible
1½ medium bell peppers, preferably red and yellow, roughly
    cut into 1-inch pieces
8 beautiful, very ripe tomatoes, cut into eight wedges each
3 medium cucumbers, peeled and cut crosswise into
    medium-thick slices
¼ cup balsamic vinegar
Salt and freshly ground black pepper, to taste

In a large bowl, combine the onion, crumbled feta, a small splash of the water the feta came in, the oil, and oregano. Mix well and let marinate 15 minutes or so to allow the flavors to mingle. Add the chopped peppers, tomatoes, cucumbers, and all the remaining ingredients. Mix well, then refrigerate for at least 30 minutes before serving. Season with salt and pepper just before serving.

SERVES 4 TO 6

Mrs. Burlette's Lobster Salad

I find it truly fascinating that a taste, a taste memory, or even just the thought of a particular recipe can conjure up such strong associations and emotional responses. This is particularly the case with this recipe, which was always prepared exclusively by Mrs. Burlette, my stepmother's mother. A truly kind soul of few words, Mrs. Burlette nevertheless had the ability to convey a sense of warmth, acceptance and welcome.

The recipe itself has an interesting history. It seems that Mrs. Burlette's mother first tasted this salad in the dining car while en route from New Orleans to California via the railroad. Obviously, she had the culinary antennae that most New Orleanians are given and promptly recognized greatness. Using her southern charm, she was able to procure the recipe, which immediately became a family tradition, always signaling the beginning of an important meal.

2 cups cooked lobster meat or shrimp (approximately two
    1¼-pound lobsters), coarsely chopped
5 large eggs, hard-cooked, peeled, yolks separated from
    whites, and whites sliced
⅔ cup distilled white vinegar
2 teaspoons salt
5 teaspoons dry mustard powder
⅓ cup olive oil
1 head iceberg lettuce
Freshly ground black pepper, to taste

In a large bowl, combine the lobster or shrimp and sliced egg whites. In another bowl, mash the hard-cooked egg yolks with a fork and stir in the vinegar, salt, and dry mustard. Whisk in the oil in a thin, steady stream until emulsified and pour over lobster or shrimp mixture. Refrigerate for 1 hour.

When ready to serve, tear the lettuce into bite-size pieces and toss well with the lobster mixture. Season with salt, if necessary, and pepper.

SERVES 4 TO 6

Asian Noodle Salad
with Sesame-Soy Vinaigrette

If you're looking for a lot of taste and not many fat calories, try this salad. I am particularly fond of Japanese *udon* noodles, but really any noodles will work just fine. This salad is equally delicious at room temperature, hot, or cold.

1 pound Japanese *udon* noodles or other pasta of choice
4 teaspoons Asian sesame oil
½ cup soy sauce, preferably low-sodium
4 teaspoons sugar
8 tablespoons sweet mirin
¾ cup rice wine vinegar
4 teaspoons canola oil
Crushed red pepper, to taste (optional)
3 tablespoons chopped fresh cilantro
3 scallions, thinly sliced on the diagonal
2 medium cucumbers, peeled, seeded, and grated
2 medium carrots, peeled and grated
Sesame seeds (optional), lightly toasted, for garnish

In a large saucepan, bring 5 quarts of salted water to a boil. Add the pasta and return to a boil, stirring occasionally. Cook, stirring occasionally, until al dente, anywhere from 7 to 20 minutes, depending on the type of noodles being used. Drain the noodles, then rinse well under cold running water, and drain again, thoroughly.

In a lidded jar, combine all the remaining ingredients except the cucumbers and carrots and shake well to blend.

In a large bowl, combine the noodles with the vinaigrette, cucumbers, and carrots and toss well to mix. Serve garnished with toasted sesame seeds, if desired.

SERVES 6

Aunt Retta's Potato Salad

Whenever we have family gatherings on my mom's side, it goes without saying that Aunt Retta will bring the potato salad. I have no recollection of any of the other eight siblings (or their spouses, for that matter) ever offering to give Aunt Retta a break. Hers is simply the best. Nothing out of the ordinary goes into it, but it is somehow the quintessential basic potato salad. This is a high honor for a southern family to bestow on one person alone, for we take our potato salad very seriously indeed, and there is nary a gathering that exists without one present. We even eat potato salad alongside gumbo! Don't ask me why, because I couldn't tell you. It's good, and that's just the way it's done.

5 pounds baking potatoes, such as Idaho, peeled and diced
1 dozen large eggs, hard cooked, peeled, and finely chopped
4 or 5 dill pickles, finely chopped, with 1 to 2 tablespoons of
    the juice reserved
1 large onion, finely chopped
2 cups mayonnaise
Salt and freshly ground black pepper, to taste

Place the potatoes in a large saucepan and add enough water to cover by 1 inch. Bring to a boil over high heat, then reduce heat to low and simmer, uncovered, until the potatoes are fork-tender, about 15 minutes. Drain in a colander and set aside to cool slightly.

In a large bowl, combine the remaining ingredients and add potatoes while they are still warm. Stir gently but thoroughly to mix. Taste and add more pickle juice, salt, and pepper, if necessary.

SERVES 8 TO 12

My Potato Salad

If you're in the mood for something a little more risqué and a bit spicier than traditional potato salad, try this recipe.

3 pounds new potatoes, scrubbed
½ small red onion, finely chopped
2 or 3 medium ribs celery, thinly sliced on the diagonal
½ medium red bell pepper, seeded and finely chopped
½ bunch scallions, finely chopped
2 tablespoons finely chopped pickled jalapeño peppers
¾ cup Basic Vinaigrette (page 198)
2 tablespoons mayonnaise
¼ cup sour cream
¼ cup minced fresh parsley
4 to 6 large eggs, hard cooked, peeled, and roughly chopped
Salt and freshly ground black pepper, to taste
8 ounces sliced bacon, cooked until crisp and crumbled

Place the potatoes in a large saucepan and add enough water to just cover them. Add a bit of salt to the water and bring to a boil over high heat. Reduce heat and boil potatoes gently until fork-tender, about 20 minutes. Drain in a colander and set aside to cool.

While potatoes are cooling, combine remaining ingredients, except bacon, in a large bowl, stirring well to mix.

Once potatoes have cooled to lukewarm, cut each into quarters and add to the bowl with the remaining ingredients. Toss gently but thoroughly to mix. Taste and adjust the seasoning.

Serve at room temperature or slightly chilled, garnished with crumbled bacon, if desired.

SERVES 6 TO 8

Salade de Susan et Philippe

When I first moved to New York City, I shared an apartment with my good friend Susan, who had been a francophile since long before I met her in the fifth grade. One evening upon returning home, I was lucky to find the remains of this salad in our refrigerator, a salad her then French boyfriend Philippe had taught her to make. That Philippe is long gone, but Susan is now happily married to another French Philippe and living the good life in Paris. We both hold this salad in high esteem and feel eternally indebted to Philippe #1 for the recipe. It is a rich salad that people love, and I often serve it at the beginning of a celebratory meal.

Orange Dijon Vinaigrette

2 tablespoons freshly squeezed orange juice
1 teaspoon grated orange zest
¼ cup red wine vinegar
2 shallots, finely chopped
1 teaspoon salt
Freshly ground black pepper, to taste
1 tablespoon Dijon mustard
½ cup extra-virgin olive oil

Salad

3 navel oranges, peeled and sectioned or cut into bite-size
    pieces
1 small red onion, thinly sliced
1 large head Boston or Bibb lettuce, rinsed, drained, and
    torn into bite-size pieces
1 bunch arugula or watercress, rinsed, drained, and cut into
    bite-size pieces
1 log (6 ounces) goat cheese, crumbled
1 ripe avocado, peeled, pitted, and cut into chunks or slices,
    as you prefer
⅓ cup pine nuts, toasted

In a small stainless-steel or glass bowl, combine the orange juice and zest, vinegar, shallots, salt, pepper, and mustard and whisk thoroughly to blend. As you whisk, add the oil in a thin, steady stream until emulsified. Set aside, covered, at room temperature until ready to assemble the salad.

In a large stainless-steel or glass bowl, combine ¼ cup of the vinaigrette with the sectioned oranges and sliced onion. Toss carefully to mix and let stand while you assemble the remaining salad ingredients.

Combine the lettuces, goat cheese, avocado, and pine nuts in a salad bowl. Add the marinated orange sections and onion slices and toss gently with enough extra dressing to coat. As Boston and Bibb lettuces are tender, don't overmix. Spoon a little extra dressing over the salad and serve immediately.

SERVES 4 TO 6

NOTE: For a more formal presentation, you can toss just the lettuces with the dressing and artfully arrange the oranges, onions, avocado, goat cheese, and pine nuts on top of the salad and around the plate border. Drizzle extra salad dressing over all.

MaMa's Shrimp Salad

Everyone makes shrimp salad in New Orleans, but as in the case of most classics, simple is best. This is a great way to begin an early dinner in the summertime, when temperatures are soaring and the cool creaminess surrounding crisp ingredients satisfies like nothing else can.

2 pounds small or medium shrimp, peeled and deveined
3 medium ribs celery, chopped
¼ medium onion, finely chopped
2 scallions, finely chopped
1 cup mayonnaise
Salt and freshly ground black pepper, to taste
1 teaspoon freshly squeezed lemon juice, or more to taste
½ teaspoon Worcestershire sauce
Lettuce leaves or 2 ripe avocados, peeled, pitted, and sliced, for serving
Sweet paprika, for garnish
1 lemon, cut into 4 or 6 wedges, for garnish

Bring a large saucepan of salted water to a boil. Add the shrimp and cook until just done. This will take only 3 to 5 minutes, depending on the size of the shrimp you are using. *Do not overcook!* Drain the shrimp in a colander and set aside to cool completely.

Meanwhile, in a large bowl combine the celery, onion, scallions, mayonnaise, salt and pepper, lemon juice, and Worcestershire. Stir well to mix.

Coarsely chop the cooled shrimp, then combine in the bowl with the mayonnaise mixture, stirring well. Refrigerate until thoroughly chilled, at least 1 hour and up to 24 hours. Taste and adjust the seasoning, if necessary, then arrange the salad on lettuce leaves or on top of sliced avocados and garnish with pinches of paprika and lemon wedges.

SERVES 4 TO 6

Spinach Salad with Warm Bacon Vinaigrette

This is a sinfully delicious salad—don't attempt making it unless you're ready for it. It is warm and rich and satisfying in a way something can be only when it's bad for you.

If you'd like to serve it as a luncheon dish or a light main-course dinner entrée, try it with just-seared sea scallops. I think it is the perfect salad to serve before Seared Calves' Liver with Balsamic Vinegar and Red Wine Sauce (page 123).

8 slices bacon
¼ cup sherry wine vinegar
1 teaspoon Dijon mustard
2 tablespoons sugar or honey
2 pounds fresh spinach, stems removed, thoroughly rinsed, drained, and patted dry, then chilled
4 large fresh button mushrooms, trimmed and very thinly sliced
½ medium red onion, thinly sliced
Salt and freshly ground black pepper, to taste

In a large enameled or other nonreactive skillet, sauté the bacon until crisp, about 5 to 7 minutes, then remove to paper towels to drain and cool. To the bacon drippings in the pan, add the vinegar, mustard, and sugar, whisking well to blend.

In a large bowl, combine the spinach, mushrooms, and onion with the hot dressing and salt and pepper. Toss well and serve immediately, with the reserved bacon crumbled on top.

SERVES 6 TO 8

Lentil Salad

Lentils are such agreeable legumes! Rather chameleon-like, they readily assume the character of whatever spices you choose to dress them up with. I find Middle Eastern spices particularly becoming to them and think that, together with the lemon and cilantro in this recipe, they make for a spicy yet light, refreshing salad that is nice on its own but would also be right at home next to grilled chicken or lamb. If you like a creamier dressing, try adding a few tablespoons of plain yogurt.

1 pound dried lentils
3 medium carrots, peeled and grated or finely chopped
1 medium red bell pepper, seeded and finely chopped
4 scallions, finely chopped
1 small red onion, finely chopped
1 medium cucumber, peeled, quartered lengthwise, and seeded
⅓ cup champagne vinegar
⅔ cup light olive oil, canola oil, or grapeseed oil
¼ teaspoon ground cinnamon
½ teaspoon ground allspice
¼ teaspoon ground cumin
⅛ teaspoon ground cloves
½ teaspoon cayenne pepper
¼ teaspoon ground coriander
2½ teaspoons salt
Grated zest and juice of 1 lemon
1 medium cucumber, peeled, seeded, and chopped
¼ cup chopped fresh cilantro

In a large strainer or colander, rinse lentils under cold running water, then transfer them to a large saucepan. Add enough water to cover by 2 inches and bring to a boil over high heat. Reduce the heat to low and simmer, covered, until the lentils are tender but not falling apart, 15 to 20 minutes.

Drain the lentils well, then rinse quickly under cold water to stop the cooking process. Drain well again, then place in a large bowl, tossing occasionally to ensure even cooling.

When the lentils have cooled to room temperature, combine the remaining ingredients except the cucumber and cilantro in a lidded jar and shake well to blend. Pour the mixture over the lentils and stir well to coat. Refrigerate the salad for at least 1 hour to chill and allow the flavors to come together.

Just before serving, add the cucumber and chopped cilantro and toss gently but thoroughly to mix. Taste and adjust the seasoning, if necessary.

SERVES 6 TO 8

Basmati and Wild Rice Salad with Dried Fruits and Toasted Walnuts

I love the flavor particular to basmati rice and the texture of wild rice. Together they create something even greater than the simple sum of their individual qualities. With the intense flavors of dried cranberries and apricots popping up to surprise you, plus the earthiness of the walnuts, this salad is a study in contrasts. It pairs well with chicken, turkey, or duck and may be eaten either hot or cold, though I believe it is most impressive at room temperature. It can be made 1 day in advance, kept covered and refrigerated until ready to serve. If making in advance, make sure to taste and reseason, if necessary.

½ cup dried apricots, coarsely chopped
¼ cup dried cranberries
½ cup freshly squeezed orange juice
1 cup wild rice
7¾ cups water
2 teaspoons salt, plus additional to taste
1 cup basmati rice
⅓ cup light olive oil
3 tablespoons champagne vinegar
1¼ cups chopped walnuts, toasted
3 scallions, thinly sliced on the diagonal
Grated zest of half an orange
Salt and freshly ground black pepper, to taste

Combine dried apricots and cranberries in a small bowl and pour the orange juice over the fruit. Let the fruits soften in the juice until ready to assemble the salad.

Place wild rice in a medium saucepan with 6 cups of the water and 1 teaspoon of the salt. Cover and bring to a boil. Reduce the heat to a low boil and continue to cook, covered, until the rice is just tender, 30 to 40 minutes.

Meanwhile, place the basmati rice in a second medium saucepan with the remaining 1¾ cups water and 1 teaspoon of the salt. Bring to a boil, stir well, then cover and reduce the heat to low. Cook 15 minutes, until the rice is tender. Remove from heat and let the rice remain in covered saucepan to steam for 10 to 15 minutes. Transfer rice to a large bowl, toss lightly with a fork and let cool to lukewarm, tossing gently periodically to cool.

While the basmati rice is cooling, drain the wild rice, rinse quickly under cold running water, and set aside to drain and cool further.

When the rices have cooled, add the wild rice, soaked dried fruits and orange juice, and all the remaining ingredients, including salt and pepper to taste, to the bowl with the basmati rice. Toss thoroughly to mix.

SERVES 6 TO 8

Salad Dressings

Basic Vinaigrette
Balsamic Vinaigrette
Blood Orange Vinaigrette
Creamy Herb Dressing
Roquefort Dressing

Basic Vinaigrette

This is just what it claims to be—a great basic vinaigrette. Wonderful on simple mesclun salads, I also like it on tender greens such as arugula, mâche, or Boston lettuce. It may also be used to dress pasta salads. I am particularly fond of Dessaux red wine vinegar, but play around with different vinegars for different tastes. The Dijon mustard you choose to use will also make a big difference in the taste. It is important to add the salt to the vinegar before whisking in the oil, as salt will not dissolve in oil. You can correct the seasoning at the end, but it's much easier if you start with a good base. This vinaigrette can be made up to 3 or 4 days in advance and kept in the refrigerator in a tightly closed jar.

¼ cup red wine vinegar
1 shallot, finely minced
¾ teaspoon salt, or to taste
Freshly ground black pepper, to taste
1½ teaspoons Dijon mustard
¾ cup canola oil

In a small stainless-steel or glass bowl, whisk together the vinegar, shallot, salt, pepper, and mustard until the salt has dissolved. While continuing to whisk, add the oil in a very thin, steady stream. Continue whisking until all of the oil is incorporated and the mixture is emulsified. Taste and adjust the seasoning, if necessary.

MAKES ABOUT 1¼ CUPS

Balsamic Vinaigrette

This is my favorite dressing for arugula. Also great on a tricolor salad (arugula, endive and radicchio) as well as with grilled or roasted vegetables. If you find yourself with a little left over, don't throw it out. It will keep for a few days in the fridge if stored in a tightly closed jar, and can add a nice finishing touch to sandwiches or pasta.

¼ cup balsamic vinegar
1 teaspoon Dijon mustard
1 teaspoon sugar
½ teaspoon salt, or to taste
Freshly ground black pepper, to taste
1 clove garlic, peeled and smashed on a cutting board with
    the side of a knife
¼ cup extra-virgin olive oil
¼ cup canola oil

In a small stainless-steel or glass bowl, whisk together the vinegar, mustard, sugar, ½ teaspoon salt, pepper, and garlic until the salt and sugar are dissolved. While whisking, add oils in a thin, steady stream until emulsified. Taste the vinaigrette along the way, as vinegars can vary greatly in strength and acidity and you may need to adjust the amount of oil accordingly. Season with salt, if needed.

MAKES ABOUT ¾ CUP

NOTE: If you're not a whisk fanatic, you can prepare this easily by placing all the ingredients in a jar with a tight-fitting lid and shaking vigorously. I usually combine the first 6 ingredients and let them sit awhile before adding the oils, allowing the salt and sugar to dissolve and the garlic flavor to permeate the vinegar. Once shaken, taste and adjust the acidity and seasoning.

Blood Orange Vinaigrette

The blood orange is a seductively alluring fruit, with whispers of red on the peel that invite us to look inside to behold just why they are named as they are. Their lusciously colored flesh is intriguing, varying from pure orange to deep, blood red, and their flavor has a certain indescribable component that regular oranges do not possess. Though they are only in season for a short time, usually late November though early March, they are worth waiting for.

I find that they are quite at home in a salad, and the recipe that follows is a delicious vinaigrette that is also low in calories, as little oil is needed to balance the acidity of the orange juice. I like to serve this on mildly flavored greens, such as Bibb or butter lettuce, red oak, or lollo rossa, with some blood orange sections included for garnish.

⅓ cup freshly squeezed blood orange juice (about 2 oranges)
1 shallot, finely minced
½ teaspoon salt
Freshly ground black pepper, to taste
¼ cup canola oil

In a small stainless-steel or glass bowl, whisk together the blood orange juice, shallot, salt, and black pepper until the salt has dissolved. While whisking, add the oil in a thin, steady stream, until emulsified. Check the seasoning before tossing with the salad.

MAKES ABOUT ⅔ CUP

Creamy Herb Dressing

Sometimes you just have to have something creamy on your greens! Inspired by an early love affair with bottled Green Goddess dressing, I find this works well on hearty lettuces such as romaine or iceberg, and it's equally good on a simple tomato and cucumber salad. Because of the egg in the dressing, proceed with caution, making sure the eggs you use come from a salmonella-free source; in any case, use the dressing the day it is made.

1 large egg
¼ cup white wine, champagne, or tarragon vinegar
1 teaspoon Dijon mustard
1 teaspoon fine sea salt
Freshly ground black pepper, to taste
1 clove garlic, pressed or minced
¾ cup canola oil
2 scallions, thinly sliced
1 tablespoon chopped fresh herb or herbs of choice (such as tarragon, parsley, chervil, cilantro, thyme, oregano, basil, or parsley) or ½ teaspoon dried herb or herbs of choice (such as herbes de Provence or Italian herb seasoning or even just basil or thyme)

In a blender, combine the egg, vinegar, mustard, salt, pepper, and garlic and process until smooth. With the motor still running, add the oil in a thin, steady stream until emulsified. Add the scallions and herbs of choice and blend again briefly just to distribute the seasonings evenly.

MAKES ABOUT 1¼ CUPS

Roquefort Dressing

Roquefort. Mmmm! One thing I absolutely cannot control myself around. I particularly love this dressing on spinach salads, with boiled eggs, crumbled bacon, and sliced red onions. It also makes a great dip for crudités.

4 ounces Roquefort cheese, crumbled
1 clove garlic, pressed or minced
2 tablespoons mayonnaise
¼ cup sour cream
½ cup buttermilk or regular milk
Salt and freshly ground black pepper, to taste

In a small bowl, whisk together all the ingredients and let stand, covered, at least 1 hour before serving.

MAKES ABOUT 1¼ CUPS

Dazzling Desserts

While desserts are certainly not a necessity, for some of us they are often the most awaited part of the meal. I have included a vast array of possibilities here, from light and easy to sinfully rich and complicated.

I am particularly partial to fruit desserts, and you will notice that fresh fruit is often highlighted in this chapter. For the recipes that call for fresh fruit, I strongly suggest that you use only the best quality fruit, most preferably while in season, as a fruit dessert can only be as good as the fruit that goes into it. When your dessert craving steers you to something comforting and creamy, there are a handful of soothing custard-based dishes (and these can even be made in advance, which is always helpful when planning a menu). And when you feel a cool finish to a meal is most appropriate, there are a number of refreshing sorbets and ice creams which are fun to make at home.

If you do decide to have dessert, I urge you to enjoy it. Life is short. Gild the lily.

Dazzling Desserts

Figs Poached in Port Wine and Cognac

Mixed Fruit Crisp

Lemon Curd Beggars' Purses with Fresh Raspberries and
Raspberry Sauce

Sautéed Peaches with Cognac and Raspberry Purée over
Vanilla Ice Cream

Daddy's Roasted Pecans

Blood Orange Sorbet

Lemon-Banana Sorbet

Watermelon Sorbet

Bananas Foster Ice Cream

Lemon Custard Ice Cream

Homemade Vanilla Ice Cream

Above and Beyond Banana Pudding

Bread Pudding with Whiskey Sauce

Coconut Tapioca Pudding

A Real Trifle

Saturday Morning Cookies

Peach, Mango, and Blackberry Tart

Basic Pie Crust

Free-Form Plum and Apple Tart with Crystallized Ginger

Sweet Potato Pie with Bourbon Praline Sauce

MaMa's Blackberry Dumplings

Peach Cobbler

Strawberry Shortcake

Banana Layer Cake

Mom's Cheesecake

Figs Poached in Port Wine and Cognac

It wasn't until I moved to New York City that I realized how fortunate I was to have access to fresh figs while growing up. I'd never thought of a fig as a luxury item before, and it was hard to believe that the majority of folks I came across here had never had a fresh fig! I was always happy when my grandmother would put on a long-sleeved shirt in the heat of a New Orleans summer and climb up into her fig tree in the backyard to harvest the figs before the birds got to them, but now I know I really had it good. We had figs and figs and figs. So many figs that MaMa usually ended up cooking some and putting them up for later.

It was this memory of MaMa cooking figs that prompted me to create this recipe one day when I learned I had people coming for dinner and not a lot of time to shop or cook. I had a bowl of fresh figs lying on the table and some ice cream in the freezer. Now I make it a point to make this regularly for dessert when figs are in season.

2 pounds fresh, firm-ripe purple figs
3 cups port
1 cup Cognac, or ½ cup Cognac and ½ cup Grand Marnier
2 strips lemon zest, 3 × 1 inches each
1 cinnamon stick
1½ cups granulated or light brown sugar, or a mixture
1 teaspoon freshly squeezed lemon juice
½ teaspoon ground allspice
¼ teaspoon ground cloves
Homemade Vanilla Ice Cream (page 220), or crème fraîche,
    for serving

Rinse figs well under cold running water, then drain and remove the coarse portion of the stem. Quarter the figs lengthwise and set aside. In an enameled or other nonreactive medium saucepan, combine the port, Cognac, lemon zest, cinnamon stick, sugar, lemon juice, allspice and cloves. Bring to a simmer over medium heat and cook until the liquid has reduced by half, about

20 minutes. Add figs and reduce heat to low. Cook until the figs have absorbed the taste and color of the poaching liquid, 10 to 15 minutes. Let the figs steep in the hot liquid 10 minutes before serving.

Serve the hot figs over ice cream, or with a dollop of crème fraîche on top.

SERVES 4 TO 6

Mixed Fruit Crisp

This is one of those classics that I don't have to bother selling you. You know that when a crisp is good, it's great. I've come across very few people who did not respond with moans of ecstasy when a truly great crisp was set before them, hot from the oven. But since a crisp can only be as good as the fruit that goes into it, it is of utmost importance that you use fruit that is at its best. The fruit should be firm-ripe. My favorite combination of fruits is below, but by all means try different combinations to suit yourself.

I make it a policy to keep extra crisp topping in plastic bags in the freezer—and when an impromptu dessert is needed, *voilà.* Just round up whatever fruit you've got lying around and top it with the already made topping. Stick it in the oven and by the time you're ready for dessert, it's ready for you. A crisp just begs to be topped with either ice cream or fresh whipped cream.

¾ cup plus 1 tablespoon all-purpose flour
8 tablespoons (1 stick) cold butter
¾ cup granulated sugar
¼ cup (packed) light brown sugar
Pinch of salt
3 Golden Delicious apples, peeled and thinly sliced
2 firm-ripe Bartlett pears, peeled, cored, and thinly sliced
4 fresh, ripe nectarines or peaches, pitted and thinly sliced
2 fresh, ripe plums, pitted and thinly sliced
½ pint fresh, ripe strawberries, rinsed and patted dry, hulled, and quartered
1 handful of ripe blackberries
1 teaspoon freshly squeezed lemon juice
Homemade Vanilla Ice Cream (page 220) or slightly sweetened whipped cream

In a medium bowl, combine the ¾ cup flour, 6 tablespoons of the butter, ¼ cup of the granulated sugar, the brown sugar, and salt. Cut in the butter with 2 knives, a pastry blender, or your fingertips until well-combined and the mixture resembles coarse crumbs. Refrigerate until fruit is ready to be topped and cooked.

Preheat the oven to 400°F.

While the oven is heating, place all the fruits in a large stainless-steel or glass bowl and add remaining ½ cup sugar, 1 tablespoon flour, and fresh lemon juice. Toss well to mix and allow to stand until the fruits begin to release their juices.

Grease a 9- × 13-inch casserole or baking dish with the remaining 2 tablespoons butter and turn the fruit mixture into it. Sprinkle with the reserved topping and bake in the preheated oven until the fruit is soft and bubbly and topping is crispy and golden brown, 30 to 35 minutes.

Serve warm, with ice cream or whipped cream.

SERVES 6

Lemon Curd Beggars' Purses with Fresh Raspberries and Raspberry Sauce

This is an exquisitely beautiful dessert, an elegant end to an eventful meal. Though it may seem difficult at first glance, all of the steps are actually quite simple and may all be prepared at least 1 day in advance and then assembled just before serving.

Lemon Curd

6 large egg yolks
1 cup granulated sugar
½ cup freshly squeezed lemon juice
8 tablespoons (1 stick) unsalted butter
1 tablespoon grated lemon zest

Beggars' Purses

9 sheets phyllo dough, about half of a 16-ounce package, thawed if frozen
8 tablespoons (1 stick) butter, melted

Raspberry Sauce

1 package (12 ounces) frozen whole raspberries
½ cup granulated sugar
¼ cup water
1 teaspoon freshly squeezed lemon juice

Garnish

1 pint fresh raspberries
Confectioners' sugar
Fresh mint sprigs (optional)

Make the lemon curd. In an enameled or other nonreactive saucepan, whisk together the egg yolks, sugar, and lemon juice. Set the pan over medium-low heat and cook for 10 to 12 minutes, whisking constantly, until the mixture is thick and coats the back of the spoon. *Do not allow to boil.*

Remove from the heat and whisk until cooled somewhat, stir in the butter bit by bit, then the zest. Place in a glass bowl or jar, cover with a sheet of plastic wrap placed directly on the surface of the curd and refrigerate until chilled and ready to use, up to 2 weeks.

While the lemon curd chills, make the beggars' purses.

Preheat the oven to 375°F.

On a clean, dry work surface, spread out one of the sheets of phyllo and carefully brush it all over with some of the melted butter (see Note). Repeat the same procedure with two more sheets of phyllo, placing each one directly on top of the first sheet before brushing it with butter.

Carefully cut the buttered phyllo stack into 4 squares of equal size, using a very sharp knife. Carefully transfer each square to a 12-cup muffin pan, and using your hands, gently press the squares into the muffin wells, tucking the centers of each square into the bottom of the wells, bringing the sides up and arranging the edges of the squares so they resemble the edges of a bunched-up pouch, taking care to leave enough space in the center so that, later, you can easily spoon in the lemon curd.

I find that you can fit between 4 and 6 purses in one 12-cup muffin pan, depending on how you choose to arrange them. There should be as much space as possible between the purses to allow for even browning and to give you enough room to get your hands around them to remove them once baked. They will be very fragile.

Once you have filled the muffin pan with as many purses as will fit comfortably, bake the purses in the preheated oven until golden brown and crispy, about 10 minutes. (While these are baking, you can prepare the remaining purses. If you have only one muffin pan, however, it is important that it be completely cooled before you place additional purses in it to bake.) When the purses are golden brown all over, and feel crispy to the touch, remove the pan from the oven and carefully remove the purses to a rack and allow them to cool completely.

If you repeat the same processes as described above with the remaining 6 sheets of phyllo, you will end up with 12 purses. Quite often some look better than others, so I typically make more than I will be needing to allow for accidents and to be able to choose the most beautiful purses to serve. Once the purses are completely cooled, they may be kept in airtight containers for 24 hours before serving.

While the final purses cool, make the raspberry sauce. Let the raspberries defrost in their pouch. Meanwhile, combine the sugar and water in a small enameled or other nonreactive saucepan and bring to a boil over medium heat. Boil for 2 minutes, then remove from heat.

When the raspberries have thawed slightly, combine in a blender with the sugar syrup and lemon juice. Process until smooth, then strain through a fine-meshed sieve into a small glass bowl or measuring cup. Refrigerate until ready to serve.

To assemble the desserts, place a tablespoon or two of raspberry sauce in the middle of a dessert plate, smoothing it out into a pool of sauce not quite as large as the plate itself.

Carefully spoon or pipe the lemon curd into the centers of the pouches, then place one pouch directly in the center of each pool of raspberry sauce. Place a few raspberries on top of the curd and some around the pouches on the plates. Sprinkle with confectioners' sugar and garnish with sprigs of fresh mint, if available. Serve immediately.

SERVES 8 TO 12

NOTE: While working with phyllo, it is important to keep unused sheets covered with plastic wrap and a damp towel over that. Otherwise, it will become too brittle to work with.

Sautéed Peaches with Cognac and Raspberry Purée over Vanilla Ice Cream

I love anything with peaches, and think this probably has a lot to do with a childhood memory I have of Mom sprinkling peach halves with sugar and sending us outside with them in the summertime. It was probably one of her tricks to get us out from under foot, but I do remember feeling very spoiled by her when she would give us peaches like this.

Later when I moved to New York City I had a real New York experience at a real New York institution: I had peach Melba at Rumplemeyer's on Central Park South. Peach Melba is such a wonderful combination of flavors and textures that I think this slight bend on the original deserves some serious attention, too.

1 package (12 ounces) frozen whole raspberries in syrup
¾ cup sugar
¼ cup water
½ teaspoon freshly squeezed lemon juice
¼ teaspoon orange extract
4 firm-ripe fresh peaches
6 tablespoons butter
½ cup Cognac
Homemade Vanilla Ice Cream (page 220)
1 pint fresh raspberries, for garnish
Fresh mint sprigs, for garnish (if available)

Let the raspberries defrost in their pouch. Meanwhile, combine ½ cup of the sugar and the water in a small enameled or other nonreactive saucepan and bring to a boil. Boil for 2 minutes, then remove from the heat.

When the raspberries have thawed slightly, combine in a blender with the sugar syrup, lemon juice, and orange extract. Process until smooth, then strain through a fine-meshed sieve into a small glass bowl or measuring cup. Refrigerate until ready to serve.

Halve the peaches, remove the pits, and cut into thin slices. In a large skillet, melt the butter over medium-high heat. Add the peach slices and sprinkle with the remaining ¼ cup sugar. Sauté until the slices are beginning to caramelize, 5 or 6 minutes, stirring frequently.

Once the slices have a nice golden brown color, pour the Cognac into the skillet and let bubble for 1 to 2 minutes, stirring, then remove from the heat.

Serve the hot peach slices over the ice cream and top with the raspberry sauce. Garnish with fresh raspberries and a sprig of fresh mint, and serve immediately.

SERVES 4 TO 6

Daddy's Roasted Pecans

Many folks roast pecans in the South, but I've never tasted any quite like this. These are great to pass around the table after dessert at Christmastime, to put out in bowls for guests, or even to give as Christmas presents.

1 large egg white
1 tablespoon water
½ cup sugar
1 tablespoon ground cinnamon
Pinch of salt
1 pound pecan halves

Preheat the oven to 225°F.

In a medium bowl, combine the egg white and water and whip to stiff peaks with a whisk or hand-held electric mixer. In another medium bowl, combine the sugar, cinnamon, and salt and mix well. Dip the pecan halves in the beaten egg white mixture, then in the sugar mixture to coat completely. Arrange on ungreased baking sheets in a single layer and bake for 1 hour, stirring every 15 minutes.

Let the nuts cool completely, then store in airtight containers for up to 2 weeks.

MAKES ABOUT 3 CUPS

Blood Orange Sorbet

The exquisite color of this fruit makes it a perfect candidate for a sorbet in the late fall through the early spring. Serve as is, garnished with a fresh sprig of mint if desired, or perhaps with a bit of Grand Marnier spooned over the top to make things just a bit more interesting.

2 cups freshly squeezed blood orange juice
½ cup sugar
¼ cup champagne, bubbly or flat
1 tablespoon freshly squeezed lemon juice

In a large stainless-steel or other nonreactive bowl, combine all the ingredients, whisking until the sugar is dissolved. Process in an ice cream maker according to manufacturer's directions.

SERVES 4

Lemon-Banana Sorbet

This is an assertive, exceedingly refreshing sorbet. I love to serve this after fish of any sort, though it also makes a nice between-course palate cleanser. Because of the intensity of the lemon juice, the banana flavor is hardly discernible, yet it serves to give the sorbet a softness it would otherwise lack, both in texture and flavor.

2 cups freshly squeezed lemon juice
1¼ cups sugar
1 large ripe banana, puréed (about ⅔ cup)

In a stainless-steel or other nonreactive bowl, whisk the lemon juice with the sugar until the sugar is dissolved. Whisk in the banana, then process in an ice cream maker according to manufacturer's directions.

SERVES 4

Watermelon Sorbet

What could be nicer than an ice-cold slice of watermelon on a warm day? How about watermelon sorbet? This is a sorbet with a very delicate flavor, and should only be made with the freshest watermelon. The lime juice serves to bring out the flavor and gives the sorbet just the tiniest tang.

If you find yourself with any leftover watermelon purée, it's great in a fruit smoothie.

5 pounds very fresh watermelon
½ cup sugar
1 tablespoon freshly squeezed lime juice
1 tablespoon cassis

Cut the flesh of the watermelon from the rind and remove all the seeds. Purée, in batches, in a food processor or blender until smooth.

In a medium bowl, combine 2 cups of the watermelon purée with the sugar, lime juice, and cassis, whisking until the sugar is dissolved. Process in an ice cream maker according to manufacturer's directions.

SERVES 4

Bananas Foster Ice Cream

Bananas Foster is a legendary New Orleans dessert, and its banana, rum, cinnamon, and vanilla flavors work well with ice cream.

1 cup milk
1 cup heavy cream
⅓ cup (packed) light brown sugar
4 large egg yolks
¼ cup granulated sugar
½ teaspoon vanilla extract
¼ teaspoon ground cinnamon
1½ cups puréed bananas (about 3 ripe bananas)
¼ cup dark rum

In a medium saucepan, combine the milk, heavy cream, and brown sugar and bring to a simmer over medium heat. While keeping an eye on the milk mixture, whisk the egg yolks together with the granulated sugar in a large bowl until thickened and pale yellow. As soon as the milk mixture comes to a simmer, slowly whisk ½ cup of the hot milk mixture into the egg yolk–sugar mixture. Add this to the simmering milk mixture in the saucepan and stir or whisk well to blend. Reduce the heat to low and continue to cook, stirring constantly with a wooden spoon, until the mixture thickens enough to coat the back of the spoon. Do not allow the mixture to boil, or the egg will curdle and the texture of the ice cream will not be smooth. Only a slight thickening is necessary.

Strain the mixture through a fine-meshed sieve into a clean bowl. Add the vanilla, cinnamon, banana purée, and rum and stir well to blend. Refrigerate, covered with plastic wrap, until thoroughly chilled, at least 2 hours, stirring occasionally. Process in an ice cream maker according to manufacturer's directions.

MAKES ABOUT 1 QUART ICE CREAM, SERVING 4 TO 6

Lemon Custard Ice Cream

If you're looking for a light, refreshing dessert but don't want anything as astringent as a sorbet, this is the perfect choice. The lemon flavor is just a foil for the rich, custard-based ice cream. A nice middle-of-the-road alternative.

2 tablespoons grated lemon zest (about 3 lemons)
½ cup freshly squeezed lemon juice
¾ cup sugar
1½ cups milk
2 cups heavy cream
4 large egg yolks
Pinch of salt

In a small stainless-steel or glass bowl, combine the lemon zest with lemon juice and sugar and let stand for at least 30 minutes.

In a medium saucepan, combine the milk and ½ cup of the heavy cream and bring to a simmer over medium heat. While keeping an eye on the milk mixture, whisk the egg yolks together with the salt until light. As soon as the milk mixture comes to a simmer, whisk ½ cup of the hot milk mixture into the yolks. Add this to the simmering milk mixture in the saucepan and stir well to blend. Reduce the heat to low and continue to cook, stirring constantly with a wooden spoon, until the mixture thickens enough to coat the back of the spoon. Do not allow mixture to boil, or the egg will curdle and the texture of the ice cream will not be smooth. Only a slight thickening is necessary. As soon as the mixture has thickened, strain through a fine-meshed sieve into a clean bowl. Strain the lemon mixture into the custard, then add the remaining 1½ cups of heavy cream and stir to blend. Refrigerate, covered with plastic wrap, until thoroughly chilled, at least 2 hours, uncovering occasionally to stir. Process in an ice cream maker according to manufacturer's directions.

MAKES ABOUT 1 QUART ICE CREAM, SERVING 4 TO 6

Homemade Vanilla Ice Cream

No matter how many flavors we can come up with, nothing can compare to real homemade vanilla ice cream. I think using a vanilla bean is key here, but if you are short on time or can't put your hands on one when you've simply got to make this ice cream, you can substitute real vanilla extract. Though I think this is a dessert in itself, it undoubtedly dresses up just about any other dessert you care to have in addition.

1 cup milk
1½ cups heavy cream
3 egg yolks
½ cup sugar
½ vanilla bean, split lengthwise
Pinch of salt

In a medium saucepan, combine the milk, heavy cream, and vanilla bean and bring to a simmer over medium heat. Make sure to scrape some of the seeds from the vanilla bean into the milk when you add it. While keeping an eye on the milk mixture, whisk the egg yolks with the sugar in a large bowl until thickened and pale yellow.

As soon as the milk mixture comes to a simmer, slowly whisk ½ cup of the hot milk mixture into the egg yolk–sugar mixture. Add this to the simmering milk mixture in the saucepan and stir or whisk well to blend. Reduce the heat to low and continue to cook, stirring constantly with a wooden spoon, until the mixture thickens enough to coat the back of a spoon. *Do not allow the mixture to boil*, or the egg will curdle and the texture of the ice cream will not be smooth. Only a slight thickening is necessary.

As soon as the mixture has thickened, strain through a fine-meshed sieve into a clean bowl. To cool the custard quickly, place this bowl inside a larger bowl that has been filled halfway with ice cubes and water. Whisk occasionally as the mixture cools. When cooled, cover with plastic wrap and refrigerate until completely chilled, at least 2 hours. Process in an ice cream maker according to manufacturer's directions.

MAKES ABOUT 1 QUART ICE CREAM, SERVING 4 TO 6 AS A DESSERT IN ITSELF OR 8 AS AN ACCOMPANIMENT TO ANOTHER DESSERT

Above and Beyond Banana Pudding

I have always loved banana pudding, but only when just made—the concept of soggy vanilla wafers just turns me off completely. If you are of like mind, you will appreciate the following recipe. It's the same idea: creamy vanilla pudding, ripe bananas, and something crispy. But the something crispy happens to be delicate lace cookies with crispy macadamia nuts. It seemed to me that a chocolate sauce was in order, too. The pudding, cookies, and chocolate sauce can all be made in advance, but the dessert itself must be assembled just before serving.

Pudding

1½ cups milk
½ cup heavy cream
½ vanilla bean, split lengthwise
4 large egg yolks
¾ cup sugar
1½ tablespoons cornstarch
Pinch of salt

Cookies

1 cup old-fashioned rolled oats
1 tablespoon all-purpose flour
¾ cup sugar
¼ teaspoon salt
1 teaspoon baking powder
6 tablespoons butter
1 large egg, beaten
1½ teaspoons vanilla extract
¾ cup chopped macadamia nuts

Chocolate Sauce

6 ounces finest-quality semisweet chocolate
2 tablespoons butter, melted
¼ cup plus 2 tablespoons heavy cream

3 or 4 ripe bananas
½ cup chopped, toasted macadamia nuts, for garnish

To make the pudding, combine the milk, heavy cream, and vanilla bean in a medium saucepan and bring to a simmer over medium heat. While keeping an eye on the milk mixture, whisk the egg yolks together with the sugar, cornstarch, and salt in a large bowl until thickened and pale yellow. As soon as the milk mixture comes to a simmer, slowly whisk ½ cup of the hot milk mixture into the egg yolk–sugar mixture. Add this to the simmering milk mixture in the saucepan. Continue to cook over medium heat, whisking or stirring constantly, until the custard has thickened and comes to a boil, about 5 minutes. Let boil, still whisking constantly, until the custard is quite thick and shiny, about 1 minute. Immediately remove the pan from the heat and strain the custard through a fine-meshed sieve into a clean bowl. To cool the custard quickly, place this bowl inside a larger bowl that has been filled halfway with ice and water. Whisk occasionally as the custard cools. Cover with plastic wrap and refrigerate until completely chilled, at least 2 hours and up to 2 days, uncovering occasionally to stir.

Meanwhile, make the cookies.

Preheat oven to 325°F. Cover one or more large baking sheets with foil.

In a large bowl, combine the oats, flour, sugar, salt, and baking powder and stir well to mix. In a small saucepan, melt the butter over medium heat. Do not let the butter color. Remove from the heat and pour immediately into the oats mixture and stir until sugar melts. Add the egg and vanilla and mix well. Stir in the macadamia nuts. Drop the batter by ½ teaspoonfuls onto the foil-covered baking sheet or sheets, spacing approximately 2 inches apart. Bake until golden brown, about 9 to 11 minutes, reversing the position of the baking sheets halfway through the baking time, if necessary. Remove the baking sheets from oven and let cool a few minutes. Remove foil from pans and, once cookies are firm, carefully peel them off the foil with your hands. You should have about 4½ dozen 3-inch cookies; if not using immediately, store them, once they are completely cooled, in an airtight container for up to 2 days.

For the chocolate sauce, melt the chocolate in the top of a double boiler over simmering water or in a glass bowl in the microwave oven. Meanwhile, combine the butter and cream in a small saucepan and heat over low heat until the butter is melted and the cream is hot, about 2 minutes. Remove from the heat and stir into the melted chocolate. Whisk until blended and smooth, then set aside until ready to serve. The sauce can be made up to a week in advance and refrigerated, covered, then reheated in the microwave or over very low heat on top of the stove.

When it's time to assemble the desserts, cut the bananas into thin slices. Spoon 2 tablespoons of the chocolate sauce in the center of each dessert plate. Arrange 5 or 6 banana slices over the sauce and center 1 cookie on top of the banana slices. Top with more banana slices and 2 tablespoons of the custard and place another cookie on top of the custard. Top again with banana slices, custard, and another cookie. Place a few more banana slices on top of this cookie and drizzle chocolate sauce over all. Garnish with toasted macadamia nuts and serve immediately.

SERVES 6

Bread Pudding with Whiskey Sauce

Bread pudding is one of the most subjective, variable desserts I know. Sometimes it's hard, sometimes soft, sometimes hot, sometimes cold, with fruit or without. And that's just the pudding part! An infinite array of toppings exists as well.

This is a composite recipe, a meeting of what I think is the best pudding and the best sauce. The pudding recipe is from my mother's good friend Miss Marie, a native New Orleanian of Italian descent who worked with Mom for over twenty years. The sauce is MaMa LaChute's recipe, which traditionally tops her whiskey pudding. The combination is simply heaven and has prompted many a religious experience among its followers. Thank you, Miss Marie and MaMa!

I think the bread pudding is best when served warm. It can be prepared without baking up to 1 day in advance (stored in the refrigerator, covered), and then put in the oven just before you sit down to dinner. Also, although I am particularly enamored of the bourbon in the sauce, it is equally delicious without the alcohol, if you prefer.

Pudding

½ French baguette (preferably day old)
4 cups milk
4 large eggs
1½ cups sugar
1 tablespoon vanilla extract
1 tablespoon ground cinnamon
4 tablespoons butter, melted

Sauce

8 tablespoons (1 stick) butter, melted
1 can (5¾ ounces) evaporated milk or ¾ cup heavy cream
1 cup sugar
1 large egg yolk, beaten
½ cup bourbon

Preheat the oven to 350°F.

Break the bread into rough pieces and place in a large bowl. Pour the milk over the pieces, mixing well. Set aside.

In another large bowl, beat the eggs, then stir in the sugar, vanilla, and cinnamon. Pour the egg mixture over the soaked bread pieces. Pour the melted butter into one 9- × 13-inch baking pan (see Note) and coat bottom and sides. Pour the excess melted butter from the baking pan or pans over the bread mixture and stir well to mix. Pour the mixture into the prepared baking pan and bake until the pudding puffs up and is set in the center, about 45 minutes. Remove from the oven and set aside until ready to serve.

While the pudding is baking, make the sauce: In a heavy, small, enameled or other nonreactive saucepan, combine all the ingredients except the bourbon and cook over medium-low heat, whisking constantly until the sauce has thickened and coats the back of a spoon, about 10 minutes. Do not allow the sauce to boil or the egg will curdle and the sauce will not be smooth. Remove from the heat, stir in bourbon, and set aside to cool slightly.

Serve the bread pudding in small bowls, with the warm sauce spooned over the top.

SERVES 8 TO 10

NOTE: Two 8 × 4-inch bread pans may also be used.

Coconut Tapioca Pudding

If you are a tapioca advocate and you like coconut, this dessert will render you speechless. It is equally delicious warm, room temperature or cold—the choice is yours. Toasted coconut is the ultimate garnish, providing a stark contrast in texture next to the smooth, creamy tapioca.

1 large egg, separated
⅔ cup granulated sugar
1 can (14 ounces) unsweetened coconut milk (available at Asian and Hispanic markets, gourmet food stores, and many supermarkets)
2 cups milk
⅓ cup quick-cooking tapioca
½ vanilla bean, split lengthwise
Pinch of salt
Lightly sweetened whipped cream, for garnish (optional)
¾ cup sweetened coconut flakes, toasted, for garnish

In a small mixing bowl, beat egg white with an electric mixer at high speed until frothy. Continue to beat, adding ⅓ cup of the sugar little by little until egg white holds soft peaks. Set aside.

In a medium, heavy saucepan combine the egg yolk, remaining ⅓ cup sugar, coconut milk, milk, tapioca, vanilla bean, and a pinch of salt. Cook over medium heat, stirring constantly, until mixture comes to a full boil, about 5 minutes.

In a medium bowl, combine egg white and tapioca mixture and cover top of tapioca with plastic wrap. Refrigerate, stirring occasionally, until pudding reaches the desired temperature.

Serve with a dollop of whipped cream if desired and top with toasted coconut flakes.

SERVES 6

A Real Trifle

My best friend growing up happened to be from England, her father having been called to New Orleans to work in the aerospace industry. Her mother made trifles often, and it was in her home that I learned about this extraordinary dessert.

I think that a well-made trifle is a work of art, and a lovely way to end just about any meal. It is important to use real sponge cake, if you have the time to make your own. Otherwise, I find ladyfingers to be the best substitute. Homemade custard is essential, and I make it a point to use quality raspberry preserves. Though traditionally served in one large, straight-sided, clear trifle bowl, I think this also lends itself to being served in individual parfait or sundae glasses, and can be made well ahead of a dinner party and simply topped with whipped cream just before serving.

Custard

2 cups milk
1 cup heavy cream
10 large egg yolks
¾ cup granulated sugar
1 teaspoon vanilla extract
2 tablespoons brandy

Spongecake

3 large eggs, at room temperature
1 tablespoon milk, at room temperature
⅔ cup granulated sugar
1 cup all-purpose flour
1 teaspoon baking powder
A pinch of salt
8 tablespoons (1 stick) butter, melted

Assembly

½ cup slivered almonds, lightly toasted
½ cup plus 2 tablespoons cream sherry

1 cup raspberry jam
2 cups heavy cream
2 tablespoons confectioners' sugar
1 pint fresh raspberries or 1 package (12 ounces) frozen
   dry-pack whole raspberries, thawed

First make the custard.

Preheat the oven to 300°F.

In a medium saucepan, combine the milk and heavy cream and bring to a simmer over medium heat. Meanwhile, whisk the egg yolks with the sugar in a large bowl until thickened and pale yellow. When the milk mixture is at a simmer, whisk it into the egg–sugar mixture, little by little, until fully blended. Stir in the vanilla and brandy, then pour the custard into a 9- × 13-inch baking dish. Place this inside a larger vessel, such as a roasting pan, and add enough warm water to reach the level of the custard in the baking dish. Cover with foil and bake in the center of the oven for 45 to 55 minutes, or until the custard is set along the edges but still slightly wobbly in the center.

Remove the pan from the oven and let the custard cool in its water bath until lukewarm. Cover the custard with plastic wrap and refrigerate until completely chilled, about 2 hours.

While custard is cooling, make the spongecake.

Preheat the oven to 375°F. Grease a 9- × 13-inch baking pan and set aside.

In a large bowl, combine the eggs and milk and beat with an electric mixer until frothy. Add the sugar and continue to beat at high speed until the mixture is quite thick and pale yellow, about 5 minutes.

In a small bowl, sift together the flour, baking powder, and a pinch of salt and fold gently into the egg mixture. Stir in the melted butter, then transfer the batter to the prepared baking pan and bake in the center of the oven until risen and golden brown, 15 to 20 minutes. Remove from the oven and let the cake cool for 10 minutes in the pan before turning it out onto a rack to cool completely.

When custard has chilled and the cake has cooled, assemble the trifle. Using a knife with a serrated edge, gently cut the cake into 1½-inch cubes. Place half of the cubed spongecake at the bottom of a large, straight-sided trifle bowl. Reserving some of the slivered almonds for garnish, sprinkle the cake with half of the remaining almonds, then with ¼ cup of the sherry. Spread ½ cup of the raspberry jam over the cake and almonds, then sprinkle with some of the raspberries and top with half of the chilled custard. Repeat the layering process and refrigerate the trifle, covered with plastic wrap, at least 4 hours and preferably overnight before proceeding.

When you are ready to serve the trifle, mix the remaining cream with the 2 tablespoons sherry and confectioners' sugar and whip until stiff peaks form. Spread over the top of the trifle and garnish with the reserved slivered almonds and any leftover fresh (only) raspberries. Serve immediately.

SERVES 8 TO 10

Saturday Morning Cookies

My mom would find the energy to whip up a batch of these on Friday nights, so that Saturday mornings upon rising we'd have an instant treat. I remember thinking how magical it seemed that you could cook things even with the oven off.

2 large egg whites
⅔ cup sugar
1 cup (6 ounces) semisweet chocolate chips
1 cup finely chopped pecans
1 teaspoon vanilla extract

Preheat the oven to 350°F. Line two baking sheets with foil and set aside.

In a large bowl, combine the egg whites and sugar and beat with an electric mixer to stiff but not dry peaks. Add the chocolate chips, pecans, and vanilla and fold in gently. Drop the batter by teaspoonfuls onto the foil-covered cookie sheets. Place in the preheated oven, then turn the oven off but leave the cookies in overnight, or for at least 8 hours, until they are crispy.

MAKES ABOUT 4 DOZEN COOKIES

Peach, Mango, and Blackberry Tart

This is a simple tart, but an outstanding combination of flavors and colors. I prefer to leave the peaches unpeeled, but if you must peel them, simply place them in a large pot with boiling water for a few minutes—the peels will slide right off.

1 Basic Pie Crust (page 233)
6 ripe peaches or nectarines
1 large or 2 small ripe mangoes
A few drops freshly squeezed lemon juice
½ cup sugar
1 tablespoon cornstarch
½ teaspoon vanilla extract
½ pint fresh blackberries
2 tablespoons butter
Crème fraîche or Homemade Vanilla Ice Cream (page 220)

Prepare the pie crust according to the instructions on page 233, rolling out the pastry and fitting it into a 9-inch fluted tart pan with removable bottom. Chill at least 30 minutes.

Meanwhile, preheat the oven to 375°F.

Halve the peaches and remove the pits. Cut the peaches into ½-inch slices. Peel the mangoes, then cut the flesh into slices of similar width directly off the flat pit. Add the lemon juice, sugar, cornstarch, and vanilla and toss well to mix. Let stand until the fruits have begun to release their juices.

Turn the fruit mixture into the chilled pastry shell. Scatter the blackberries on top, dot with the butter, and bake 45 minutes to 1 hour, or until the fruit is bubbly and lightly brown around the edges, and the pastry is golden brown.

Remove the tart from the oven and let cool on a rack for at least 20 minutes before removing the sides of the pan and serving. Serve warm with a dollop of crème fraîche, or with the ice cream.

SERVES 8 TO 10

Basic Pie Crust

This is just what it claims to be. It is the recipe I use for almost all of my pies, and can be varied to suit savory fillings as well, as noted below. It is actually very simple to make, and though I realize that pie crusts can be a source of intimidation for many cooks, I urge you to give this a try. The only thing to be careful of is to not to overwork the dough. The recipe can be doubled in direct proportion to accommodate a pie that also has a top crust. I actually have a lot of fun handling the pastry, crimping edges decoratively, etc. For this you don't need any special gadgets, only your hands and perhaps a knife and a fork. Experiment and have fun.

1¼ cups unbleached all-purpose flour
¼ teaspoon salt
¼ cup superfine or granulated sugar
8 tablespoons (1 stick) unsalted butter, cold, cut into pieces
1 large egg yolk, beaten with 2 tablespoons cold water

In a food processor, combine the flour, salt, and sugar and pulse just to mix. Add the butter and process until the mixture resembles coarse crumbs. While the processor is running, add the beaten egg yolk–water mixture in a slow drizzle through the feed tube until the pastry begins to come together into a ball. Do not over process or the pastry will be tough. Remove the pastry from the workbowl and pat together with hands, working the dough as little as possible. Shape into a smooth, flat disk, dust lightly with flour, and wrap in plastic. Refrigerate for at least 1 hour and up to 1 day, or freeze for up to 2 months.

When ready to use the pastry, remove from the refrigerator and let it warm up a bit before attempting to roll it out. On a lightly floured surface, roll the pastry out approximately ⅛-inch thick. Transfer the pastry to the pie plate or tart pan to be used (see Note) and carefully fit it in, gently easing the pastry against the bottom and sides and leaving a ½-inch overhanging the top edge if a decorative border is desired.

Flute the edges of the pastry in the pie plate and return the pastry shell to refrigerator for at least 30 minutes before filling and baking according to the recipe.

MAKES ENOUGH PASTRY FOR ONE 8- OR 9-INCH PIE CRUST

NOTE: I find the easiest way of transferring the pastry to the pan is to use the flat, removable bottom of a tart pan. You can easily slide this under the rolled out pastry, as it has no edges or bumps to get in the way. Just pick up the pastry with the tart pan bottom and gently lay it in the tart pan, if that's what you're using, or slide it off the pan bottom into your pie plate. Then use your hands to gently fit the pastry into the pan or plate and smooth out the corners and edges.

VARIATION: If you need a crust for something savory, such as Chicken Pot Pie (page 114) or Crawfish Pie (page 92), simply omit the sugar and increase the salt to 1 teaspoon. Follow all other directions as for the sweet pastry.

Free-Form Plum and Apple Tart with Crystallized Ginger

I love the rustic look of this tart. Made without a pie plate or tart pan, the pastry is folded over the fruit to make its own sides. With sugar sprinkled over the rough, folded edges, it makes a beautiful end to any meal.

> 1 recipe Basic Pie Crust (page 233)
> 6 sweet apples, such as Golden Delicious
> 1 teaspoon freshly squeezed lemon juice
> 3 ripe plums
> ¼ cup chopped crystallized ginger
> ½ cup plus 3 tablespoons sugar
> 1 tablespoon cornstarch
> 1½ tablespoons butter
> 1 cup crème fraîche, for garnish (optional)

Preheat the oven to 375°F.

Prepare the pie crust according to the directions on page 233. Roll the pastry out to a 15-inch circle. Instead of fitting it into a pie plate or tart pan, however, transfer it to an ungreased flat baking sheet. Let sit in the refrigerator or another cool place while you assemble the remaining ingredients.

Peel and core the apples. Cut into ¼-inch slices and toss in a large stainless-steel or glass bowl with the lemon juice.

Halve the plums and remove the pits, then cut as well into ¼-inch slices. Add to the bowl with the apples, along with the ½ cup sugar, chopped crystallized ginger, and cornstarch. Toss well to mix, and let stand 3 or 4 minutes, until the fruits have begun to release some of their juices.

Transfer the fruit to the rolled out pastry, leaving a 2-inch border all around. Turn any sharp edges of the fruit so they will not tear the dough when you fold it up. Carefully fold the edges of pastry up over fruit filling, taking care not to tear the dough.

Lightly brush the upper edges of pastry with water and sprinkle with the 3 tablespoons sugar. Dot the fruit with the butter and bake in the center of the oven until the fruit is bubbly and the pastry is golden brown, 45 minutes to 1 hour.

Remove the tart from the oven and let it cool, on the baking sheet, on a wire rack. When ready to serve, carefully slide the tart from the sheet onto a serving platter, using one or two wide metal spatulas to help. Serve warm or at room temperature, with a dollop of crème fraîche on the side, if desired.

SERVES 6 TO 8

Sweet Potato Pie with Bourbon Praline Sauce

This is my homage to Omar, otherwise known to many New Orleanians as "The Pie Man." And that he was. *The* pie man. To this day I've yet to taste a sweet potato or coconut custard pie as this man could make. You would happen upon him when you were least expecting it, usually while combing the Quarter or sometimes at a stand at the Jazz Fest or any other number of regular places he haunted. As he was exceedingly humble and discreet, if you didn't know the treasures held within that basket or unassuming sack, you could easily pass him or any of his disciples by without a second glance. He did not have to advertise: Those who knew his talent knew it well. It always seemed demand far outweighed supply, for I don't think there was ever a time that I happened across a full stock. You took what was left, knowing it would be unspeakably delicious and well worth the gamble.

I can't claim to know any of his secrets, and there must have been many of them—probably ones too simple to figure out. But I have worked on my version of this memory and it brings me back there, not quite all the way, but then, I'm not Omar...

Unlike regular potatoes, which turn gummy, sweet potatoes may be processed in a food processor or whipped with an electric mixer and the result is pure smoothness.

1 recipe Basic Pie Crust (page 233)

Filling

1½ cups mashed or puréed cooked sweet potatoes
½ cup (packed) light brown sugar
1 teaspoon ground cinnamon
½ teaspoon salt
½ teaspoon ground nutmeg
½ teaspoon ground allspice
¼ teaspoon ground cloves

2 large eggs
1 teaspoon vanilla extract
½ cup evaporated milk
4 tablespoons butter
¼ cup freshly squeezed orange juice

Sauce

2 cups sugar
½ cup water
1 cup pecans, chopped or left whole, as you prefer
¼ cup plus 1 tablespoon heavy cream
1 tablespoon unsalted butter, cold
¼ cup water
1 tablespoon bourbon
½ teaspoon vanilla extract

Preheat the oven to 450°F.

Prepare the pie crust according to the directions on page 233 and fit the rolled-out pastry into a deep 9-inch pie plate, leaving a ½-inch overhang. Crimp the edge of the pie shell decoratively. Refrigerate until ready to use, at least 30 minutes.

Meanwhile, make the filling. Combine the sweet potatoes, sugar, cinnamon, salt, nutmeg, allspice, cloves, eggs, and vanilla in a large mixing bowl. Beat with an electric mixer until thoroughly blended and smooth.

In a small saucepan, combine the evaporated milk and butter and stir over medium heat until the milk is steaming and the butter is melted. Remove from the heat and stir into the sweet potato mixture along with the orange juice. Pour the mixture into the prepared pie shell and bake at 450°F for 10 minutes. Reduce the heat to 350°F and continue to bake until the filling is set and a knife inserted in the center comes out clean, about 45 minutes. When the pie is done, remove from the oven to a rack to cool.

While the pie is baking, make the sauce. In a very clean stainless-steel saucepan, combine the sugar and water and cook over high heat, never stirring, until the syrup begins to color around the edges. If during this process sugar begins to burn on the sides of the pan, wipe the sides of the pan with a clean (this is important) pastry brush that has been dipped in cold water. When the syrup is a medium amber color around the edges, swirl the pan to mix (*do not stir*) and continue to cook until all the syrup is a medium amber color.

Remove the pan from the heat. Add the pecans and swirl to mix well. Add the heavy cream little by little (*be careful, as mixture is likely to splatter at this point*), then return the pan to low heat and cook until the cream is absorbed into the syrup and the sauce is smooth. Add the butter and stir until melted and blended in. Carefully add water, bourbon, and vanilla and stir well. Remove from the heat and let cool, stirring occasionally (see Note).

Serve the sauce warm over the warm or room temperature pie, with a dollop of whipped cream on the side.

MAKES ABOUT 1½ CUPS SAUCE, ENOUGH FOR 1 PIE SERVING 8 TO 10

NOTE: If you are making the sauce in advance, store it in a covered jar in the refrigerator when cooled. It will keep at least 3 weeks if stored this way. When you are ready to use it, simply heat, uncovered, in a microwave oven.

MaMa's Blackberry Dumplings

MaMa LaChute used to warn us incessantly about the snakes in the black-berry bushes over the levee, yet she herself has never had any qualms about tromping through the bushes herself to gather enough blackberries for dumplings. She simply walks out of her front door and, crossing the street, begins climbing the levee, and once she gets to the other side will walk along until coming to a patch of blackberry bushes. I guess she knows all the good spots by now. She must be on first-name basis with all the snakes at this point, and perhaps they admire her sense of purpose and simply get out of her way, knowing she doesn't disturb them unless a calling has been made for these dumplings, one of her previously well-kept secrets.

Perfect Biscuits (page 160)
3 pints fresh blackberries
3 cups sugar
4 cups water
Juice of ½ lemon
1 teaspoon vanilla extract
4 tablespoons butter
Crème fraîche, Homemade Vanilla Ice Cream (page 220),
    or whipped cream, for garnish

Prepare the dough for the biscuits and set aside.

In a medium saucepan, combine the blackberries with the sugar, 3 cups of the water, and lemon juice and cook until the berries are soft and a heavy syrup has formed, about 15 minutes. Remove from the heat and strain off the syrup from the berries, setting the berries aside with ½ cup or so of the syrup and return-ing the remaining syrup to the saucepan.

Add the remaining 1 cup water, the vanilla, and the butter to the syrup in the saucepan. Bring to a boil over medium-high heat, then drop the reserved biscuit dough by the tablespoonful, in batches, into boiling syrup and cook until the dumplings float to the surface, indicating they're cooked through, about 5 minutes.

Serve the dumplings immediately, in small bowls with some of the hot syrup spooned over them. Spoon some of the cooked berries over the dumplings at serving time. Serve garnished with a dollop of crème fraîche, ice cream or whipped cream.

SERVES 4 TO 6

Peach Cobbler

So very southern, so very good, peach cobbler should only be made in the thick of summer with the most beautiful ripe peaches you can find. Though it's perfectly delicious on its own, I usually serve it with vanilla ice cream or with lightly sweetened whipped cream.

Topping

2 cups unbleached all-purpose flour, plus a bit more for
   rolling out the dough
1 teaspoon baking soda
1 teaspoon cream of tartar
6 tablespoons sugar
½ teaspoon salt
2 tablespoons unsalted butter, cold
2 tablespoons vegetable shortening, cold
¼ cup heavy cream
½ cup milk

Peaches

10 medium ripe peaches, halved, pitted, and thinly sliced
1 cup sugar
1 cup water
2 tablespoons cornstarch
1 teaspoon freshly squeezed lemon juice
1 teaspoon vanilla extract
2 tablespoons butter
Homemade Vanilla Ice Cream (page 220) or slightly
   sweetened whipped cream

In a large bowl, combine the flour, baking soda, cream of tartar, 4 tablespoons of the sugar and salt. Cut in the butter and shortening with a pastry blender, two knives, or your fingertips until the mixture resembles coarse crumbs. Add the cream and milk and stir just to combine. Do not overwork the dough. If the mixture seems very wet and sticky, add a bit more flour. Pat dough into a flattened disk, wrap with plastic wrap and refrigerate until ready to bake the cobbler, at least 1 hour.

Meanwhile, preheat the oven to 350°F.

In a small bowl, stir the water, cornstarch, and lemon juice until blended. In a large saucepan, combine the peaches and sugar and stir over medium-high heat to dissolve the sugar. Stir the cornstarch mixture into the peaches and cook until the peaches have softened and the juices are slightly thickened, about 7 minutes. Remove from the heat and stir in vanilla and butter. Pour mixture into a 9- × 13-inch baking dish and set aside while you roll out the biscuit topping.

Remove the biscuit dough from the refrigerator and roll out on a lightly floured surface to a thickness of ⅜ inch, in the shape of the baking dish containing the peaches. Carefully transfer the dough to the baking dish, easing in the sides. Sprinkle with the remaining 2 tablespoons sugar and bake until the topping is puffed and golden brown, 25 to 30 minutes. Serve hot or warm with vanilla ice cream or whipped cream.

SERVES 8 TO 10

Strawberry Shortcake

Real strawberry shortcake is one of the all-time great classic southern desserts. A close kin to peach cobbler, the real thing is prepared with buttery biscuit shortcakes and nothing else but ripe strawberries that have been talked into releasing their juices by a little sugar. Topped off with lightly sweetened whipped cream, the result is ambrosial.

Strawberries

3 pints ripe strawberries, rinsed and patted dry, hulled, and sliced
1¼ cups granulated sugar
1 teaspoon grated orange zest
½ teaspoon orange extract

Shortcakes

¼ cup granulated sugar
1 cup cake flour (not self-rising)
1 cup unbleached all-purpose flour
1 teaspoon cream of tartar
1 teaspoon baking soda
½ teaspoon salt
6 tablespoons unsalted butter, cold, cut into pieces
½ cup heavy cream
¼ cup plus 1 tablespoon milk

Garnish

2 cups heavy cream
3 tablespoons confectioners' sugar
Fresh mint sprigs (optional)

Preheat oven to 375°F.

Combine the strawberries with the sugar, orange zest and orange extract. Let macerate at room temperature until serving time, or at least 30 minutes.

To make the shortcakes, combine the sugar, flours, cream of tartar, baking soda, and salt in a large bowl and stir well to mix. Using a pastry blender, knives, or your fingertips, cut the butter into the flour mixture until it resembles coarse crumbs. In a small bowl, combine the heavy cream and milk and stir into the butter-flour mixture until just incorporated. Do not overmix, or the shortcakes will be tough. Gather the dough together and place on a lightly floured surface. Roll out to a thickness of ¾-inch, and using a 3-inch biscuit or cookie cutter or the rim of a glass, cut out the dough. Gather dough scraps together and knead briefly to recombine; reroll and cut dough. Place on an ungreased baking sheet and bake for 12 to 15 minutes, or until risen and golden brown. Remove to a rack to cool.

While the shortcakes bake and cool, whip the cream with confectioners' sugar in the bowl of an electric mixer to soft peaks and refrigerate until ready to serve the shortcakes.

When you are ready to serve the shortcakes, cut them in half horizontally and place one bottom half on each dessert plate. Spoon the strawberries over the shortcake bottoms, allowing some of the released juices to moisten the biscuit. Top the strawberries with a large dollop of whipped cream, then replace the top of the shortcake and serve immediately, garnished with fresh mint sprigs, if desired.

SERVES 6 TO 8

Banana Layer Cake

This is a delicious cake that everyone loves. Make it a day ahead of time if possible, as the cake becomes more moist as it sits. Just remember that it should be kept refrigerated because of the cream cheese icing.

Cake

1½ cups sugar
1 cup mashed bananas (about 3 bananas)
½ cup vegetable oil
2 large eggs
¼ cup buttermilk
1 teaspoon vanilla extract
2 cups unbleached all-purpose flour
1 tablespoon baking soda
½ teaspoon salt
1½ cups chopped pecans

Frosting

1 pound (3¾ cups) confectioners' sugar
8 tablespoons (1 stick) butter, at room temperature
8 ounces cream cheese, at room temperature
1 large ripe banana, mashed
½ cup chopped pecans

Preheat the oven to 350°F. Grease and flour two 9-inch round cake pans.

In a large bowl, combine the granulated sugar, 1 cup mashed bananas, oil, eggs, buttermilk, and vanilla and beat with an electric mixer to blend thoroughly. Sift the flour, baking soda, and salt into the banana mixture and beat until well blended. Stir in the pecans. Divide the batter between the prepared cake pans and bake in the center of the oven for 25 to 30 minutes, or until a toothpick inserted in the center of a layer comes out clean. Let the layers cool in the pans for 5 minutes, then turn out onto racks to finish cooling.

While the layers are cooling, make the frosting. In the bowl of an electric mixer, beat the sugar and butter with the electric mixer until very light and fluffy. Add cream cheese and banana and beat until blended and smooth. Stir in the pecans.

When the cake layers are completely cooled, place one on a serving plate and spread with some of the frosting. Top with the second layer and spread the remaining frosting over the sides and top.

SERVES 10 TO 12

Mom's Cheesecake

Though I have been many places and had many cheesecakes, this is still my favorite. It is highly likely that there is an emotional link, but I don't think that this clouds my perception of this being a truly great dessert. I love the fact that there is no crust, no textured otherness to interfere with the smooth, creamy cheesiness of this cheesecake. The sour cream topping is an amazing contrast, and acts to lighten the overall effect.

It is important to start with cream cheese that is warm enough to blend very smoothly with the remaining ingredients. Also, take care not to overbake, or you will have something that resembles scrambled eggs around the edge of your cheesecake. Otherwise, it's simple as pie.

2 packages (8 ounces each) cream cheese, at room
    temperature
4 large eggs
1¼ cups sugar
1 teaspoon vanilla
2 cups sour cream
½ teaspoon almond extract

Preheat the oven to 250°F.

In a large bowl, combine the cream cheese, eggs, ¾ cup of the sugar, and the vanilla and beat with an electric mixer until very smooth and light. Pour the mixture into an ungreased 9-inch springform pan and bake for 45 minutes, or until set in the center. Remove to a rack to cool for 15 minutes, leaving the oven on.

In a medium bowl, combine the sour cream, remaining ½ cup sugar, and the almond extract and stir well to blend. Pour the mixture over the warm cheesecake, then return the cake to oven and bake 15 minutes longer. Remove from the oven and cool completely on the rack. Refrigerate for at least 4 hours or overnight, until completely chilled. Remove the sides of the pan before serving.

SERVES 10 TO 12

Index

About the Author

CHARLOTTE ARMSTRONG credits her culinary inspiration to her Cajun and southern grandmothers and her New Orleans upbringing. A graduate of the French Culinary Institute, she cooked at New York City's Aquavit restaurant for three years. Charlotte is currently a private chef in New York City.